Coastal Walks
in
CORNWALL

Eleanor Smith

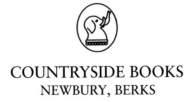

COUNTRYSIDE BOOKS
NEWBURY, BERKS

First published 1983
by Frederick Warne Ltd

This completely revised and updated edition
published 2002

COUNTRYSIDE BOOKS
3 Catherine Road
Newbury, Berkshire

To view our complete range of books,
please visit us at
www.countrysidebooks.co.uk

ISBN 1 85306 739 3

Front cover photo of Tintagel, taken by Bill Meadows

Produced through MRM Associates Ltd., Reading
Typeset by Techniset Typesetters, Newton-le-Willows
Printed by Woolnough Bookbinding Ltd., Irthlingborough

Contents

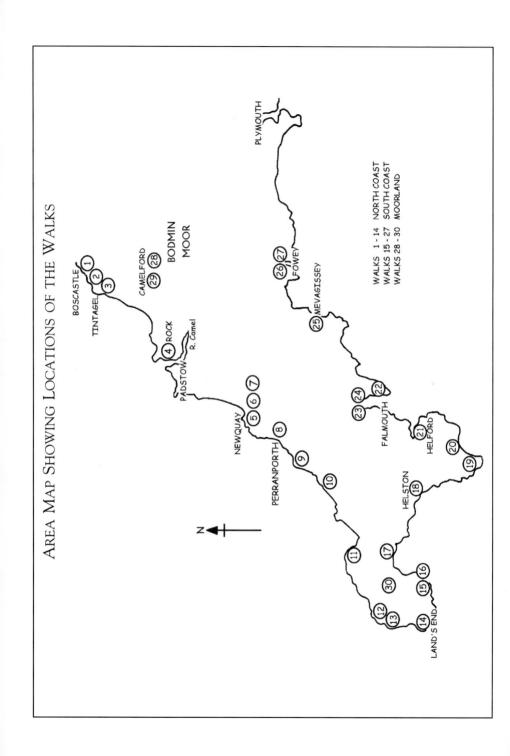

AREA MAP SHOWING LOCATIONS OF THE WALKS

WALKS 1 - 14 NORTH COAST
WALKS 15 - 27 SOUTH COAST
WALKS 28 - 30 MOORLAND

WALK

Publisher's Note

We hope that you obtain considerable enjoyment from this book; great care has been taken in its preparation. Although at the time of publication all routes followed public rights of way or permitted paths, diversion orders can be made and permissions withdrawn.

We cannot of course be held responsible for such diversion orders and any inaccuracies in the text which result from these or any other changes to the routes, nor any damage which might result from walkers trespassing on private property. However, we are anxious that all details covering the walks are kept up to date and would therefore welcome information from readers which would be relevant to future editions.

The simple sketch maps that accompany the walks in this book are based on notes made by the author whilst checking out the routes on the ground. However, for the benefit of a proper map, we do recommennd that you purchase the relevant Ordnance Survey sheet covering your walk. Ordance Survey maps are widely available, especially through booksellers and local newsagents.

Introduction

Cornwall, a county almost surrounded by water, must offer some of the best coastal walking in the country. The river Tamar rises four miles inland from Marsland Mouth on the north coast and flows south to reach the sea at Plymouth forming the boundary of Devon and Cornwall. The Atlantic Ocean rolls in to the north coast and the English Channel to the south.

The geology of Cornwall makes this a county of vast contrasts. The country rock of slate has been intruded upon by the granites of Bodmin, Carnmenellis and Madron Moors, while the serpentine rock which forms the Lizard area has a long history and may have been formed beneath an ocean, millions of years ago.

The china clay district of St Austell consists of decomposed granite forming the mineral kaolin. This valuable commodity, used in so many items of daily life from paint to medicines, is the backbone of Cornish industry today. The intrusion of the granites caused the mineralisation of these areas which, from prehistoric times, has occasioned the rise and fall of the fortunes of this unique county.

In the years between the 15th and 19th centuries, hundreds of small mines were operating, producing vast quantities of tin, copper, lead and associated minerals. The collapse of this industry came with the discovery of alluvial deposits in the Far East which could be extracted more cheaply.

Immense fortunes were amassed by the mineral lords during the heyday of Cornish mining and the reminders of past glories are with us today in the properties and possessions of these people, now mostly in

the care of the National Trust. Coastal walking in Cornwall will bring this part of history to mind as small ports and harbours, built to bring in the coal and export the ore, are visited during the walks.

I am an inveterate coastal walker, be it wet and windy or calm and sunny. I never tire of the same walk as each season offers its own variations and the sea is forever changing. I hope that you who use these walks will feel that Cornwall can still be a place in which to 'get away from it all'. Your car can take you so far but the true beauty-spots can only be found by walking to discover the coasts of Cornwall.

All the walks described here are on official rights of way. Cliff paths are subject to erosion and detours may have to be made, particularly after a stormy winter. Much of the coastline comes under the care of the National Trust and is usually well-signposted. It is never wise to use the coastal footpath during a gale. Strong winds can make walking a real hazard and gusts of up to 100 mph have been recorded.

Vast stretches of golden sands and sheer cliffs are beautiful to look at, but the walker must watch for a fast incoming tide. It cannot be stressed too strongly that one never walks round a jutting headland at beach level on a rising tide. Plan your walk around the tide chart, readily and cheaply available at most newsagents.

Good, stout, waterproof boots and thick socks are advisable, both for comfort and to help to avoid the twisted ankles that can occur, particularly when walking with inadequate footwear over wet rocks. A good waterproof is another necessity since storms from the Atlantic blow up very suddenly. Although the sketch maps in this book should be sufficient, the relevant Ordnance Survey Explorer map is given at the beginning of each walk as well as the name of the nearest town used as a starting point.

The walks in this book are suitable for the average person who likes a moderate ramble. Yet cliff paths can be steep and, while attention has been given to avoiding the worst of these, some of the lesser ones are included where places of special interest are involved. A note is made of this before any walk incorporating any steep ascent or descent. Children over the age of eight should be able to cope with most of the walks and parents prepared to carry a young one in a papoose-type sling should manage very well. I would not feel it advisable to take a toddler or a pushchair on any coastal walk given here.

With this in mind, do take your time, your camera and binoculars and enjoy all that Nature has to offer in this lovely county of Cornwall.

Finally, my thanks go to my family for their help in this project, particularly to my husband Joe and sons Andrew and David.

Eleanor Smith

BOSCASTLE

Length : 4 miles

Getting there: Leave Camelford by the B3266, following the signposts for Boscastle. This road enters the village down a very steep hill and the panorama before your eyes as you enter the village is quite breathtaking.

Parking: The car park is just past the harbour on the right.

Map: OS Explorer 111 (GR 210910).

Boscastle harbour and village, nestling at the foot of some of the highest and most spectacular cliffs in Cornwall, are now a sleepy holiday area, very different from the bustling places they must have been until the early years of this century. From here the slate extracted from the Delabole Slate Quarry was exported. This quarry still exists today and the large hole in the ground, one mile in circumference, is evidence that for the past 700 years this industry has been operating. There were boatyards, sail lofts and a forge in the harbour area but they are now a youth hostel, gift shop and café. It is here that the river Valency crossed by a new bridge – the old one having been swept away in floods in 1957 – makes its way down to the sea.

During this walk you will see evidence of the old 'stitch' field system. Each plot being a narrow field of early medieval date. You will also be able to visit Forrabury church. Legend has it that a set of bells was being brought by sea to be placed in the tower of the church. After a pilot boarded the ship to navigate the narrow entrance into Boscastle harbour, a terrific storm sprang up. The ship bounced about on the massive waves but was mercifully intact when the storm abated. The pilot sank to his knees to thank God for their deliverance but the captain said, 'You should be thanking me, not God for bringing us to safety'. Whereupon, a huge wave engulfed the ship and it sank with all hands. Be the legend true or false, the fact remains that Forrabury church is still without a ring of bells. There are some who say, however, that at certain tides the sound of bells can be heard mournfully pealing just off the rocks close to the church.

FOOD and DRINK

The Cobweb Inn in Boscastle was first licensed in 1790 and has many historical artefacts on display. It serves food and drink all day. Telephone: 01840 250278.

THE WALK

❶ The walk starts along the harbour. Keep to the left-hand side, carefully passing the bollards and mooring ropes, until you reach the ancient jetty built in 1584.

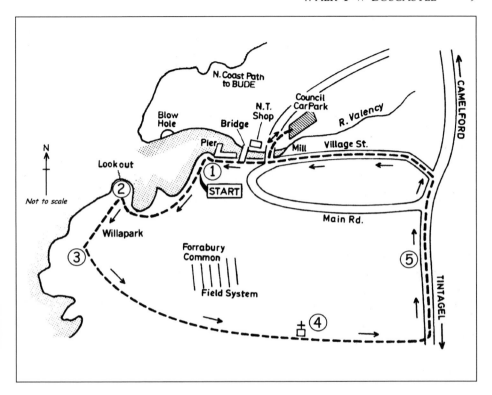

Nearly opposite the jetty is the outer bar, originally built in the late 1700s but blown up by a Second World War mine and rebuilt by the National Trust in 1962. Look for the 'blow hole' here. At the right state of the tide, water will rush through the hole eroded by the sea, through the cliff and emerge as a fountain, making an awesome noise.

❷   The path wanders over the cliff, uphill, but there are some welcome seats placed very strategically. Take a look at the sturdy little look-out tower on the headland of Willapark. The view from here is superb. To the north is Bude Bay, Hartland Point and Lundy Island. To the south can be seen Tintagel and Trevose Head. The cliffs are sheer and there are warning notices of undercutting. This is some of the finest cliff walking in north Cornwall. It is said that it was here that Sir Henry Irving received the inspiration to conceive the setting for one of his London productions.

❸   Take the left-hand path leading inland from the headland across Forrabury Common. Here you will see the ancient field system. Continue to the church which stands proud ahead of you. Notice the old cross in the churchyard and the weather vane in the form of a fish.

❹   Leave the churchyard by the main

Boscastle

gate. Walk downhill to the T-junction. This is the main road so take care. Cross over to the lane almost opposite signed 'Village Only'. A particularly pleasant walk now follows, passing picturesque old cottages. After the Methodist Chapel, the row of houses you come to on the right is built on the site of the old Bottreaux Castle, the castle of Boscastle.

❺ The field just beyond the last of the houses takes on a semi-circular formation and dips sharply into the valley. Here is the site of the original earthen mound or motte on which the castle was built. Continue on through the village, noting the water wheel as you pass, to cross the bridge and so back to the car park.

NECTAN'S GLEN AND ROCKY VALLEY

Length : 3 or 4 miles

Getting there: From Camelford, take the well-signposted B3263 for Tintagel. On reaching Tintagel, follow the sign for Bossiney and Boscastle. Just through Bossiney the road goes steeply downhill, round a sharp bend, then uphill.

Parking: On the left, near the top of the hill it should be possible to park in a lay-by almost opposite the start of the walk. For Rocky Valley take your car back down the hill. On the wide bend at the bottom of the hill there is a lay-by on the left

opposite the sign to Trevillet Mill and the walk. If you plan to eat at the mill, it should be possible to leave your car there.

Map: OS Explorer 111 (GR 075892).

This walk cannot, strictly speaking, be called a coastal walk but I feel that I may be excused for including it in this book since it has been established that as early as 1799, travellers regarded the then-called 'Nathan's Cave' as one of the natural wonders of Cornwall. This later became known as Nectan's Kieve, 'kieve' being the Cornish word for a cauldron, bowl or basin – a name aptly used for the fall of water into a 'kieve'. The height of the fall is about 50 ft dropping first into a granite basin, then through a rock cavity for its final fall into another stone basin and into the river. It is quite spectacular in its situation among overhanging trees and bushes.

A house from which refreshments can be obtained stands at the entrance to the fall. A charge is made for the final descent to the waterfall. The owners have made the conservation of the area of special importance.

The valley is properly called Millcombe, but the top half is now called Nectan's Glen and the lower part, Rocky Valley.

Both walks are quite unique. The walk down Rocky Valley is beside the rushing water of a trout stream. The old buildings are the remains of mills. About halfway down, just before crossing a bridge, take a look around a derelict building which was once a woollen mill, the walls of which were built against the rock face. As the buildings gradually crumbled through the years of disuse, most unusual carvings became exposed. Unique to Cornwall, they are cut into the slate behind the fallen granite wall of the mill. They are Bronze Age 'Maze' carvings some 3,000 years old. Other engravings may be awaiting discovery among the confusion of rocks in this valley. Nobody can possibly know the origin of these markings but they are of Middle Eastern design and could have

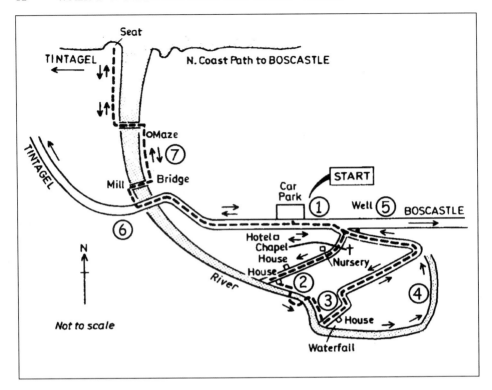

been the work of shipwrecked sailors who whiled away the winter months in this valley, repairing their boat ready to put to sea again in the spring.

THE WALK

❶ Start the walk to the left of the large flat conversion. The track is wide and

---

FOOD and DRINK

Trevillet Mill is open all year from 11.30 am to 9 pm and boasts a 15th-century mill-wheel inside. Full meals and snacks are available. Telephone: 01840 770564. Refreshments at the café, which stands at the entrance to the waterfall, are available from Easter to the end of October.

---

signed Nectan's Glen. In a few yards notice the ancient holy well on the left which is dedicated to St Piran, the patron saint of Tinners as is the adjacent chapel. Turn right past the chapel. The drive, wide now and tarmacked leads to a few houses which are passed before entering the woods and valley. Keep to the right all the way.

❷ On entering the woods the path can be slippery but is well-defined. Do not take the first bridge which crosses the stream but continue on the left-hand bank crossing over on the next two bridges. The path leads gradually uphill and can be rather muddy in places.

❸ At the top of the hill are the remains

Nectan's Glen

of a house. Continue on, bearing to the right and eventually reaching a fence and gate. This is where the entrance to the falls and the tearoom can be found.

❹ To return, either follow the path through the wood or use the lane which services the one or two cottages above the glen. Although this route is slightly longer than the woodland path, the less sure-footed will probably prefer it to the down-ward journey through the wood.

❺ On reaching the road it is advisable to move your car to the lay-by opposite the path into Rocky Valley.

❻ Pass Trevillet Mill and keep to the signed route crossing a bridge, following the well-defined path towards the sea. It was here that the bird, the Cornish Chough, once nested. Rare and unusual flowers can still be found in this sheltered place.

❼ Pause to look here at the carvings before you continue to walk down the valley to the sea. At high tide the roar is deafening as the water enters the gorge. Climb the path up the cliff on the left for a wonderful coastline view. The return walk is up the valley, retracing your steps.

TINTAGEL

Length : 3 miles

| **Getting there:** Leave Camelford by the B3263, signposted for Tintagel. The road twists and turns but is well signed all the way to Tintagel, approximately 10 miles. | **Parking:** There are plenty of car parks at Tintagel. A good one is opposite the Old Post Office in the main street. | **Map:** OS Explorer 106 (GR 053883). |

Tintagel, known the world over for its association with the legendary King Arthur and the Knights of the Round Table, is a place to be visited during the comparatively peaceful months of spring or autumn. It is a mecca indeed for tourists and its popularity can cause some minor inconveniences in July and August.

The village itself is small and it straggles along one main street where cafés and gift shops hold pride of place. However, a good example of Tudor building may be seen in the Old Post Office, now owned by the National Trust. This was a manor house of the period and has an attractive well-preserved interior and a peaceful garden.

The castle building was begun by Reginald, Earl of Cornwall in the 12th century and completed by King Richard II. It has served as many things in its time, including a prison but it is not surprising that it has succumbed to the effects of several centuries of erosion in this exposed place. The castle is now in the care of English Heritage.

Beyond the castle is an isthmus known as 'The Island'. Recent archaeological research suggests that between AD 420 and AD 600 there were around 1,000 persons living there in 150 little houses. Even more interesting is that Roman design drainage was incorporated in these structures. It is also believed that tin was smelted here and that trading was carried out with Mediterranean countries. This headland site was fitting for a stronghold with its narrow neck to the mainland. It certainly earned John Leland's title of 'unbeatable'.

From the headland are some of the most dramatic cliff views of the north coast. The cliffs provide a suitable home for the buzzard and kestrel and a variety of other sea birds. Rock samphire and thrift are among many attractive plants common to this part of the coast.

Barras Head, a promontory facing the castle was the first place in Cornwall to be given to the National Trust. Much of the Cornish coastline is now in their care but, in 1894, when speculative building was just beginning, it was thought that this

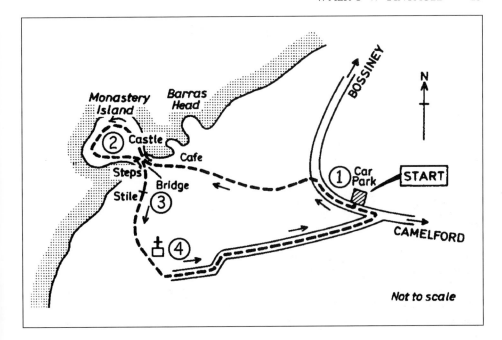

beautiful headland was to be the next site for a hotel. Much concerned at this, a group of artists raised the then princely sum of £505 by public subscription, purchased the land and gave it to the National Trust.

During this walk you will pass the church of St Materiana. It was built during the time of the first Norman Earls of Cornwall. The stone coffin of unusual length with a beautifully carved cross on the lid is probably of the time of Edward I.

THE WALK

❶ Assuming that you have left the car opposite the Old Post Office, turn right into the main street. You will soon see a sign on the left for the castle. Take this rough track going steeply downhill towards the beach. Keep to the main track all the way. On reaching the path just above the beach, pause to look down. If the tide is low, walk into the cavern known as Merlin's Cave, running under the island. To proceed any further you will now need to pay an entrance fee.

❷ The approach to the Norman castle is over the bridge and up some steps into the outer ward. Pass through the gateway into the ruins and walk through the castle area into the recently excavated island site. Notice the well, the chapel and the walled garden.

❸ After leaving the island and recrossing the bridge, take a path leading to a flight of very steep steps. Climb these to the inner ward of the castle. Keep to the right where, very soon, a sign to the church will be seen. Take any of these paths towards the church which lies just ahead.

Tintagel

❹ After leaving the church through the main door, turn left on to a metalled road away from the coast. Walk along this road which bears left after a short distance and runs steeply downhill, passing various houses en route. The road then goes uphill and joins the main street not far from the car park.

While this walk is not long, the interest it has to offer may tempt the walker to explore further and spend more time on it than a three mile walk usually takes.

FOOD and DRINK

There are many cafés and pubs to be found in Tintagel. One of the best is Ye Olde Malthouse in Fore Street. Telephone: 01840 770461.

DAYMER BAY

Length : 3 miles

Getting there: Leave Wadebridge by crossing the bridge over the river Camel. At the roundabout turn left, then left again, signed Rock, Polzeath, etc (B3314). After about 5 miles turn left for	Rock and Pityme. Do not go into Rock village but take a right turn just past a pub called the Pityme, signed Polzeath. After about a mile turn left for Daymer Bay.	**Parking:** In the car park at Daymer Bay. **Map:** OS Explorer 106 (GR 929778).

Daymer Bay, an expanse of sand just in the Camel estuary, is a paradise for children with its sand dunes, firm beach and sheltered situation. However, it is in an estuary and care should be taken if bathing. The famous, or rather infamous, Doom Bar, which stretches across the mouth of this estuary has been the cause of many ship-wrecks. It is a stretch of sand which has formed over the years and now effectively blocks the entrance to Padstow harbour for large ships. The area is an important one for birdwatching and the dunes support a wide variety of wild flowers.

The little Norman church of St Enodoc, which is one of the points of interest along this walk, was buried in the sand for many years. It was called locally 'Sinkininny' and when a service was held once a year, access had to be made through a skylight by the vicar and churchwarden. The church was restored in the 19th century and services are now held there regularly. It is unusual in having a steeple which is slightly crooked.

Rock is well-known as a sailing centre. It lies almost opposite Padstow from which there is a ferry service. Padstow is the scene, on May Day every year, of the 'Obby 'Oss festival, an ancient pagan ceremony associated with fertility rites. It attracts large crowds nowadays although originally it was just a village celebration.

THE WALK

❶ After parking the car, walk back up the lane a few yards looking carefully for a sign on the right for St Enodoc church. The path is wide and passes between some lovely houses and gardens. In a short while it narrows and crosses a bridge.

❷ Follow the white-painted stones which lead to the church. You are now on the golf course. Look out for golf balls! After leaving the church, bear right along a shallow valley alongside a stream still following the white stones. Cross a small footbridge by a pond and bear left up a track.

❸ On reaching a tarmac road cross it,

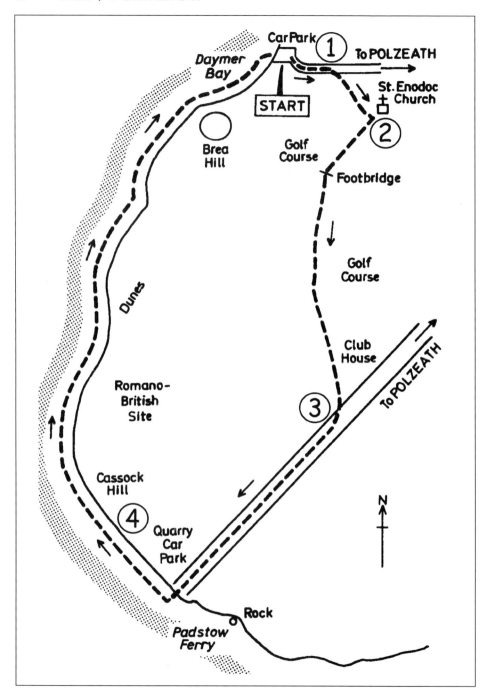

Daymer Bay

diagonally, to pass through the bushes onto a path. Continue to follow white posts or stones across the golf course. This path joins the Club House drive at the end of which, turn right downhill into Rock.

❹   The walk back depends on the tide. If it is low, then enjoy the walk along the beach all the way back to Daymer Bay. If it is high or rising, then it is as well to follow

FOOD and DRINK

At Rock you will find the Rock Inn. It is open all day and food is available from 12 noon to 2.30 pm and from 7 pm to 10 pm. Telephone: 01208 863498. There is also a café at Daymer Bay which is open during the summer months.

the marked coastal path through the sand dunes, parallel with the shore.

NEWQUAY AND WATERGATE BAY

Length : 5¹/₂ miles

Getting there: Approaching Newquay from the north on the A392, turn right onto the A3058 at the roundabout at Quintrell Downs. Go over the level crossing and continue until	you reach Narrowcliff. Just after a sign on the left marked 'Railway Station', turn left and you will see a car park almost immediately on the left.	**Parking:** In the car park as above. **Map:** OS Explorer 106 (GR 814619).

The walk begins at the major holiday resort of Newquay, a busy town which developed from a very small fishing village known as Towan Blystra. The inhabitants of the village spent their time catching shoals of pilchards which invaded the area of Newquay Bay during the autumn months. The fish were then salted and prepared for export to Latin countries to be eaten during Lent. For some reason, during the late 19th century, the pilchards failed to follow their usual routes and the fishing industry fell into decline. Mackerel and shell fish are still caught in Newquay Bay, however, and fishermen augment their income by taking holidaymakers on sight-seeing and fishing trips during the summer months.

It was fortunate that the decline in the fishing industry coincided with the arrival of the railway in Cornwall as this enabled the county to welcome more visitors and brought a new way of life to the local people.

Newquay has seven of the most beautiful beaches in the county. The Atlantic Ocean laps its shores making it a surfer's paradise and the golden sands a child's dream. A detour can be made here to explore Porth Island (Trevelgue Head). This promontory fort offers many interesting features. The bank and ditch fortification is thought to be one of the best preserved in the country. There is a large Bronze Age barrow dominating the headland and a spectacular blow-hole in the left-hand angle of the rocks.

THE WALK

Note: If you propose to walk on the beach, in either direction, consult the tide table and allow yourself three hours before high water. If you do use the beach, it is very necessary to watch the tide carefully.

❶ After leaving your car, walk back to the main street (Cliff Road). Turn right towards the Great Western Hotel. Continue along the footpath parallel with the beach below. On reaching a shelter at the end of the promenade, turn left towards the sea. Bear right across the open cliffs, an area known

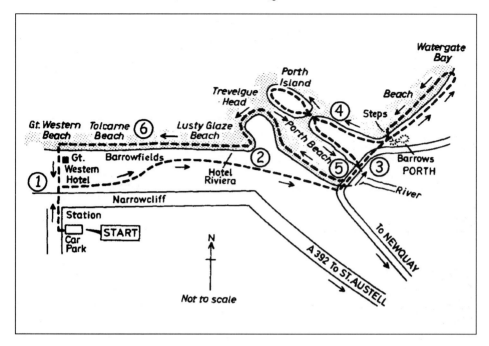

as the Barrowfields. This name is self-explanatory as the barrows are much in evidence.

❷ On reaching the Hotel Riviera, bear left, then turn left at the road junction. Follow the road, then the footpath down to Porth Beach. Walk across the beach keeping close to the wall as the river crossing is only possible by the road.

❸ After crossing the river, continue on the pavement, uphill, until you reach a coast path sign. Take this path and follow it all the way to Watergate Bay, passing two large barrows en route.

❹ The walk back to Newquay is along the beach. Just before reaching a bridge joining Porth Island to the mainland, climb a steep flight of steps from Whipsiderry Beach to the coast path above as it is very difficult to negotiate the rocks beneath the bridge and tidal conditions can be dangerous. Walk down the hill to a pitch and putt course. At this point you can make the detour around Porth Island.

❺ Returning to the beach do not attempt

FOOD and DRINK

Lookover Cottage Tearoom and Garden, in delightful surroundings close to Porth Beach, offers breakfasts, lunches, teas and snacks all day. The food is freshly prepared and the tearoom is open March to the end of October. Telephone: 01637 876725.
Watergate Bay has a variety of hotels and a beach restaurant where food is available when Lookover Cottage is closed.

Watergate Bay

to walk seawards around the rocks to Lusty Glaze Beach, instead follow the outward path to Lusty Glaze.

❻ If the tide is very low, descend the steps to beach level. The way should now be clear and the walking easy across the wide open, sandy beaches. Tolcarne is the next one followed by Great Western. Walk up the slope to the left of the beach and emerge onto a footpath a few yards from the Great Western Hotel and so back to your car.

NEWQUAY AND EAST PENTIRE

Length : 3¹/₂ miles

Getting there:
Approaching Newquay from the north on the A392, turn right onto the A3058 at the roundabout at Quintrell Downs. Go over the level crossing and continue until

you reach Narrowcliff. Just after a sign on the left marked 'Railway Station', turn left and you will see a car park almost immediately on the left.

Parking: In the car park as above.

Map: OS Explorer 106 (GR 814619).

A second walk in the Newquay area is well worthwhile as the town has much to commend it. Newquay has a history of great enterprise going back to the 16th century. This route will take you along the old tramway, now known as the Tramtrack leading between two hotels to the harbour. It was along this route that the minerals were carried after being transported from the south coast. It was constructed in the early 19th century by the then local squire named Trefrye. This enterprising man also built the quay in the centre of the harbour to facilitate the loading and unloading of the trucks. This quay was joined to the mainland by a wooden structure supporting the tramway. The Great Western Railway used parts of the old tramway when bringing the railway to Cornwall. The track now being used in this walk is all that is left of it in Newquay today.

Newquay was originally called Towan Blystra and it was in the 16th century that Bishop Lacey gave the money for the construction of a new quay to provide a

harbour; from this the name Newquay evolved.

The harbour houses an inshore lifeboat, much used during the summer months to rescue intrepid holidaymakers. The adjacent rowing club accommodates the gigs; long rowing boats now used only for competition racing. In the early part of the last century they were still being used as pilot boats to guide ships safely into harbour.

You will pass the Huer's Hut en route, so called from the pilchard-fishing days. A

FOOD and DRINK

Newquay has a wealth of pubs, cafés and restaurants. The Central Inn in Central Square is an interesting town centre pub where you can watch the world go by! Telephone: 01637 872195. The Lewinnick Lodge on East Pentire headland has magnificent views from its terraced gardens and serves food all day. Telephone: 01637 878117. A café at Fern Pit overlooking the river Gannel is open during the summer months. Approach this from the headland via a rough road.

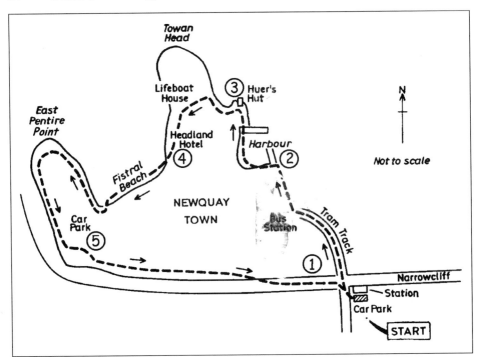

'huer' would scan the bay for the shoals of pilchards approaching the shores during the months of August to October. On sighting the fish he would alert the village with a cry of 'Heva, Heva'. The boats would then be launched and encircle the shoal with a seine net. When the fish were brought to the beach, the rest of the inhabitants would help to land them and cure the catch for storing for their own use during the winter or for export.

THE WALK
❶ Leave the car park and walk into the main street where, immediately opposite, is the tramway track between two hotels. On reaching a grassed area known as the Killacourt, overlooking Towan Beach, take any of the paths across. If the tide is low, then descend the steps to the beach and turn left towards the harbour wall. If the tide is high, then follow the footpaths skirting the beach and take the signs for the harbour.

❷ On reaching the harbour take a look at the lifeboat and the gigs. If the tide is low, walk across the beach; if not, climb the hill, turn right at the top into Fore Street and then turn right at the Red Lion inn and so join the path leading from the harbour. Continue seawards along the tarmac road, at the end of which is a flight of steps. Ascend these and on reaching the open cliff take any of the paths across the clifftop aiming for the white building ahead. This is the Huer's Hut.

Newquay

❸ Pause here and enjoy the views across the bay right to the lighthouse at Trevose. After leaving the hut, follow the tarmac road, or use the cliff path if you prefer, and join a clearly defined route towards the old lifeboat house, car park and Towan Head. It is worth walking out on to the headland for the wonderful views. You can see Fistral Beach, famed for international surfing contests. Take the footpath in front of the Headland Hotel, a landmark from Victorian times. It is usually possible to walk across the beach at any state of the tide but there is a path through the dunes, if preferred.

❹ After crossing the beach, ascend a flight of steps on to a road. Turn right here and use the road which gradually deteriorates into a track, passing hotels and houses on your left. Continue walking uphill until reaching an open space and car park. This headland is known as East Pentire. The views across Crantock beach to the left and the river Gannel estuary are superb.

❺ The walk back into town is necessarily through the built-up area of East Pentire. This has compensations as the footpaths are wide and the district very pleasant. In about a mile you will reach a roundabout. Turn left here, then take the first right into Crantock Street. This will take you back to the town centre where you retrace your steps to return to the car park.

CRANTOCK AND PORTH JOKE

Length : 4 miles

Getting there: Leave
Newquay on the A3065
towards Redruth. Take the
first right turn after crossing
Trevemper Bridge over the
river Gannel. Turn right at the
next crossroads and then

first right into Crantock
village. Keep left on reaching
the village square, taking the
road signposted 'To the
Beach'.

Parking: In the National

Trust car park adjacent to the
beach.

Map: OS Explorer 104
(GR 788609).

This walk combines not only a variety of
terrain but delights the eye with its
colourful and scenic views. You will see
huge sea caverns where the colours in the
slate are quite beautiful. These rocks were
formed during the Devonian Period
approximately 350 million years ago. The
quartz veins running through them were

Crantock

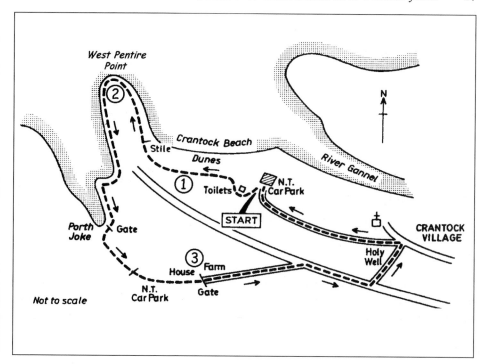

produced at the time of the granite intrusion.

You will see Bronze Age barrows on Cubert Common. Legend has it that if any of these are disturbed, disaster will befall the village of Cubert. Strangely enough they are still intact so perhaps legend has its uses after all.

The National Trust cares for sections of this walk. Porth Joke is one area where, even in the height of the season, one can enjoy reasonable seclusion, no doubt due to the absence of any amenities.

Crantock village deserves more than a glance. The church is noted for its exceptional carvings, both on the screen and bench-ends. Take a look at the stocks at the side of the church and the unusual stone coffin in the churchyard. There are two holy wells in the village: one in the village centre and one, dedicated to St Ambrose, halfway down the road to the beach. Surfers make full use of this beach though the river Gannel flows into the sea here which can make for dangerous tidal conditions.

THE WALK

❶ Leave the car park by the path behind the toilets. Keep left at the top of the hill as there is a maze of paths leading through the dunes towards the beach which do not make for comfortable walking. In about half a mile the dunes give way to farmland and the path skirts the edge of two cultivated fields. The view from here is superb. The path now descends by steps to a footbridge, then, uphill, bearing left. At a junction of

On the walk

paths keep right. Pass in front of the Crantock Bay Hotel.

❷ Keeping always to the path nearest to the sea, continue to the headland known as West Pentire Point. There is nice springy turf to walk on here, with an easy path down into Porth Joke. Cross over the footbridge and take the path leading to the left and inland which leads to Cubert Common.

❸ At a gate and National Trust car park turn left onto a wide track. In about quarter of a mile the track ends with a gate leading to a tarmac road. Turn left

FOOD and DRINK

The Albion Inn in Crantock is everything an old inn should be. There is good food and drink with cosy log fires in winter. Telephone: 01637 830243. The Bowgie, passed en route at West Pentire, is another welcoming inn offering a variety of well-prepared food. Telephone: 01637 830363.

and continue uphill to a T-junction. Turn right and take care as this is a busy road. Take the first left turn. This road leads back into Crantock village. The walk ends with a gentle downhill stroll back to the car park.

PERRANPORTH

Length : 6¹/₂ miles

Getting there: Leave Newquay on the Redruth road, the A3065. On reaching Goonhavern after about 8 miles, turn right to Perranporth. Follow this road into the town and at the crossroads, turn right towards the sea.

Parking: The car park adjacent to the beach is the most convenient one to use.

Map: OS Explorer 104 (GR 760544).

Perranporth, famed for its two miles of sandy beaches, is an active holiday resort. Its vast expanse of sand is used for beach sports and the Atlantic waves for surfing. The beach is backed by a range of sand dunes which stretch for miles. Among them is the lost church of St Piran. This oratory, buried under the sand, was uncovered due to the shifting of the sand during the 19th century. It is believed to be one of the oldest church buildings in Britain, being of the 6th century. With its exposure to the elements it began to deteriorate very quickly, a deterioration helped by human hands seeking souvenirs. The little church was eventually protected by a concrete shell which afforded suffi-

cient cover until 1981 when there was further encroachment by both sand and water. After much discussion the parish council decided to re-bury it and only a cross now marks the spot where this lonely church lies hidden.

THE WALK

❶ Take the road leading uphill over the cliff to a car park at the top. Walk diagonally across this towards Droskyn Castle, now private apartments. Turn right behind the Castle where there is a wide track. In a few metres you will see the coast path sign. Here there is a choice of paths. Take the wider inland path or the coast path. These join at a stile and steps. Continue on the coastal path towards Cligga Head.

❷ This area is a site of geological interest which produced a variety of minerals attracting geologists from many countries. Tin was mined here. Note the capped shafts. Now it is a rather desolate place with remains of buildings used during the last war. A glider and light aircraft base is

---

FOOD and DRINK

A variety of pubs and restaurants are available in Perranporth. Buttercups café is conveniently situated in the centre of the town. It offers light meals and is open all year. Telephone: 01872 572311. Refreshments are also available at the Blue Hills Tin Stream Works. Open all year. Telephone: 01872 553341.

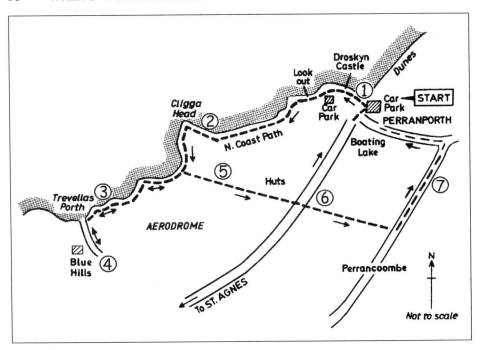

situated on the headland where concrete paths lead across the heath.

❸ Leaving Cligga behind, the path is easily defined, with spectacular views towards St Agnes. On reaching Trevellas Porth, a pretty spot with a pebbly beach, though unsafe for bathing, make a short detour. Here you will find the Blue Hills Tin Stream Works. A guided tour will show how tin has been streamed here for hundreds of years.

❹ The return route necessitates retracing your steps to Cligga Head. From here take any of the paths across the headland making towards the airfields and sheds. Continue to the road, which can be quite busy, cross over and take the footpath opposite, signed to Perrancoombe. This half-mile field path makes a pleasant downhill walk to the village. At the road, turn left and walk the short distance back to the car park.

CHAPEL PORTH

Length : 3 miles

Getting there: From Redruth, take the A30 road to Bodmin until you reach a busy roundabout where there is a Little Chef and petrol station. Turn left onto the B3277. The approach to the village passes the museum on your left just before a left turn for Chapel Porth. Continue to follow the signs to the Porth where the approach road is steep and narrow. You will notice the words Chapel Porth outlined in white stones on the cliffside.

Parking: In the National Trust car park which is almost on the beach.

Map: OS Explorer 104 (GR 698495).

This is Cornwall's north coast at its most spectacular. The cliff area is steep, rugged, and littered with mining remains. The village of St Agnes is well worth a visit, particularly the church and the Railway Inn. During re-flooring work in the church in 1931, traces of early structures were revealed, probably a pre-Norman chapel. The pub is famed for its collection of shoes. There are all kinds and dozens of them, from dancing shoes to clogs. The beach for St Agnes, known as Trevaunance Cove, is about a mile from the village and is very popular during the summer. St Agnes Beacon, which dominates the area is a high granitic outcrop, hence the mineralisation of the surrounding area. Bonfires are lit here on special occasions. It is said that it is possible to see 30 church spires on a clear day from this point.

THE WALK

❶ Start by ascending the steep cliff path from the road with the sea on your left. The path is easily defined and the views are superb. It goes downhill after a while and crosses a small stream. From here keep to the left. Do not take the wide track leading off to the right. Climb up the next cliff, which is rather steep but the view from the top makes it very worthwhile. Follow the coast closely and continue walking until an engine house is reached.

❷ This is the engine house for the Towan Roath shaft of Wheal Coates mine and has been restored by the National Trust. It also forms the frontispiece for Daphne Du Maurier's book, *Vanishing Cornwall*. Continue on the coast path until reaching a car

---

FOOD and DRINK

St Agnes village offers a variety of pubs and cafés. The Driftwood Spars, a comfortable pub and hotel offers a wide selection of food and drink. Telephone: 01872 552428. A National Trust café, situated in the car park of Chapel Porth, provides snacks and speciality cakes and ice cream. Open every day during summer and weekends only in winter.

Wheal Kitty mine

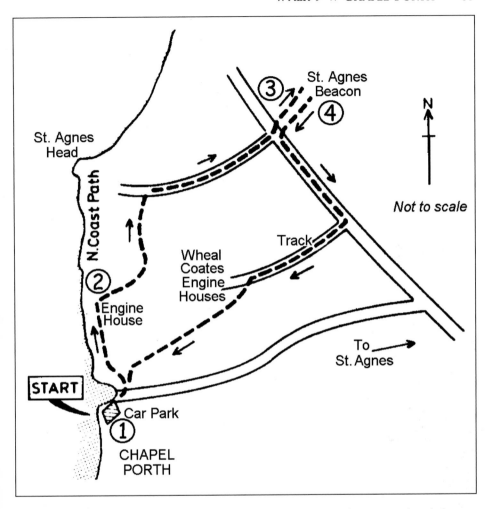

park. Turn right along a footpath and join the tarmacked track leading to the road. Cross over and take the path almost opposite leading to the top of the beacon.

❸   A good steady climb is rewarded with marvellous views: the rugged coastline on one side and on the other inland views reaching across to the distinctive outline of the china clay district. Carn Brea, another granitic outcrop, surmounted by its castle and monument, dominates the skyline in the near distance.

❹   Use the same path to descend from the beacon. On reaching the road, turn left and walk for about half a mile until reaching a track leading off to the right. This is rough but wide and leads down to Wheal Coates. Just before reaching the mine buildings, bear left and follow the track all the way back to Chapel Porth.

PORTREATH AND PORTHTOWAN

Length : 7 miles

Getting there: Take the B3330 out of Redruth or leave the A30 at a sign for Portreath. Either route will take you along the valley to the village. Turn right at the Portreath Hotel.

Continue to the top of Lighthouse Hill.

Parking: In the car park at the top of Lighthouse Hill.

Map: OS Explorer 104 (GR 660464).

This walk is steeper and longer than most and should, therefore, only be attempted by the more experienced walker.

Portreath is a small holiday village now, but in times past was an important harbour for this part of the north coast. It was known as Bassett's Cove, after the family of prominent mineral lords of the district who established the harbour to export tin and copper ore, and import coal. Minerals were carried by pack mules until 1810 when the horse-drawn tramway was established. This was closed down about 1870, by which time copper exports had ceased. Part of our walk is along the old mineral railway track. Before leaving the village take a look at the harbour and notice the day-mark known locally as the 'Pepper Pot', on the cliff.

A day-mark is a tower, and day-marks vary much in shape according to their location. Some of them are very high, for example, the one at Gribbin Head where it commands an important site marking the entrance to St Austell Bay and to Fowey. Another, at Stepper Point where it marks the entrance to Padstow harbour, looks almost like an engine house chimney. The 'Pepper Pot' is much smaller, is painted white and is indeed shaped just like a pepper pot. It marks the entrance to Portreath harbour – and acts as a guide to shipping in the area. The name 'day-mark' is used as these towers do not have lights and so cannot be confused with a lighthouse with its navigational beam.

THE WALK

❶ Join the coastal path immediately and walk downhill passing the 'Pepper Pot' on the way. Turn left at Portreath Hotel into Sunnyvale Road. Continue for about 500 yards to a granite post on your left. An engine house and direction arrows are carved on the stone. Join the old tramway at this point.

❷ The track is easy to follow and well signed. It supports a wealth of wild flowers along the hedgerows. At a fork where you will find some houses, take the lower or right-hand path. It crosses a road and a

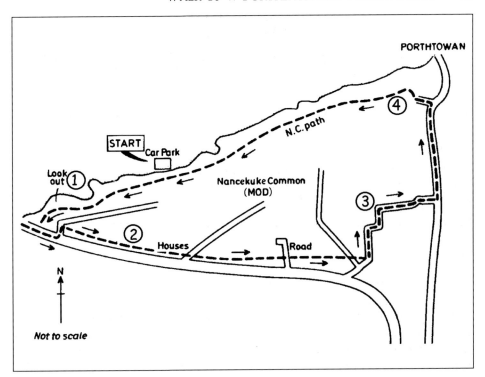

lane before emerging onto a tarmac road. Carry on taking the higher road. At the junction turn left. Follow this lane uphill.

❸ At the top of the hill the road bends sharply right and begins to descend, turning left, then right. Halfway up the next

---

FOOD and DRINK

The Waterfront Inn at Portreath has a pleasant patio area overlooking the beach and is a good place to enjoy well-cooked food. Telephone: 01209 842777. The Avalon Restaurant and Tearoom in Porthtowan is open all day during the summer though winter times may vary. Breakfast, lunch, evening meals and snacks are available. Telephone: 01209 890751.

---

slope turn left and follow this road passing an old school house on the way. Turn right here. At the next junction, the main road, turn left. Continue to Porthvean Road on your left. N.B. If you wish to walk into Porthtowan village, continue downhill ignoring Porthvean Road and join the coast path for the return route from there.

❹ Continue along Porthvean Road which soon becomes a wide track. Look for a sign to Factory Farm. A wide, stoney track passes the buildings and leads to the coast path. From here you will skirt the Ministry of Defence property with the sea on your right and some spectacular views. The path leads directly into the car park.

CARBIS BAY AND ST IVES

Length : 4 miles

Getting there: Leave the A30 Redruth-Penzance road at the end of the Hayle bypass, taking the signs for St Ives. Follow these signs for about 3 miles until you reach Carbis Bay. Look for a	turn on your right, signed Carbis Bay church, and turn into Porthrepta Road. Pass the church on your left and almost immediately turn left into a free car park.	**Parking:** In the free car park mentioned above. **Map:** OS Explorer 102 (GR 530387).

This walk uses firm and sheltered paths and is, therefore, very suitable for a windy or damp day. You will experience spectacular views across to Godrevy lighthouse and the river Hayle estuary. Take the

opportunity to visit the Tate St Ives Gallery overlooking Porthminster Beach. Artists in all mediums, both past and present, are well represented here.

The narrow streets, the abundance of

Godrevy lighthouse

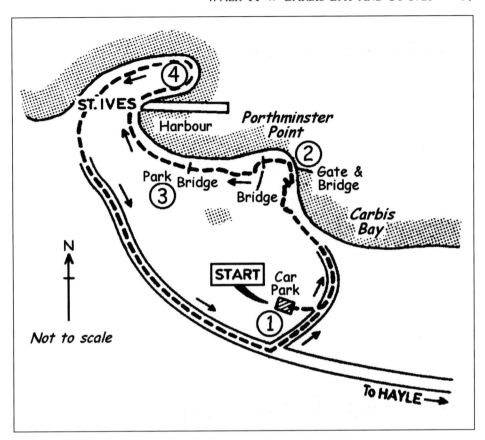

ST. IVES
④
Harbour
Porthminster
Point
Park Bridge ←
③
Bridge
② Gate &
Bridge
Carbis
Bay
N
↑
Not to scale
START Car
Park
①
To HAYLE →

flowers, the colourful boats moored along-side the quay all play their part in the enjoyment of this unique town.

Your approach on the A30 Hayle bypass will cross the river Hayle estuary, a well known bird-watching spot. You will almost certainly see heron, black-headed gull, oyster catchers and other waders.

THE WALK

❶ Make your way downhill to Carbis Bay beach. Keeping to the path above the beach, walk through a private car park, pass over a bridge and up a flight of steps.

The view of the bay here is quite spectacular. Continue uphill until reaching a road. Turn right passing between several attractive houses.

❷ At a sign 'Pedestrians Only' on the right, take the path downhill to a five-barred gate on the right. This has a National Trust plaque marking Porth-minster Point. Pass over a low granite stile beside the gate then under a railway bridge. The path here is to the right but after a few yards take a left fork onto the coastal path. Keep to the top path nearest to the railway line. At another bridge turn left and cross the bridge over the railway. Turn right past a house called Vy and Carrack. Turn right immediately after this house, taking the lower concrete path to Porthminster beach, passing over a metal bridge en route.

❸   Take a path through the gardens. At the end of the gardens do not ascend the steps but keep straight on into an area known as The Warren. You will now pass many typical artists and craft studios as you approach the harbour area.

I would not presume to guide you through the town. Sufficient to say that wherever one looks there is something unusual and very individual. Walk out on to the island with its little fisherman's chapel or on to Smeatons Pier where you can fully appreciate how St Ives became an artists' paradise.

FOOD and DRINK

The Sloop Inn on the harbourside is the oldest inn in the town with an interesting history. Food is served all day with many local dishes on offer. Telephone: 01736 796584. There is also a café on Porthminster beach where refreshments can be enjoyed during the summer months.

❹   The walk back has to follow the same route unless road walking is preferred. If this is so, then just follow the signs for Carbis Bay. However, in retracing your steps along the coast, small variations can be made. If it is low tide, you can cross the beach at Porthminster and make another deviation a little further on. Do not cross the railway bridge at the top of the hill above the beach but keep straight on until the original drive is joined once again.

LEVANT AND BOTALLACK

Length : 3 miles

Getting there: Take the B3306 from St Just, signposted for Morvah and St Ives. At Trewellard, take the left turn in the centre of the village,

which leads down to Levant Mine.

Parking: There is ample space on the clifftop near the mine.

Map: OS Explorer 102 (GR 365345).

This part of Cornwall is in the heart of the deep mining area. It has seen the rise and fall of many enterprises and has witnessed serious disasters. The Engine House at Levant Mine where this walk begins, was the scene of a tragic accident on 20th October 1919. The cap on the engine above ground snapped and 31 men who were being brought up the shaft in a cage, hurtled to their death below ground. Now in the care of the National Trust it is possible to enter this engine house which also has 'Steaming Days'. Telephone: 01736 786156 for details.

Attempts at modern mining have been made but economic pressures forced their closure. They have, however, left behind a legacy of museums in one of which, at Geevor Mine, it is possible to venture underground. For opening times, telephone: 01736 788662.

As you progress along the coast and reach Botallack you will see the spectacular Crowns engine houses. They have inspired many artists and photographers and it is easy to see why, especially when viewed against the backdrop of a full

blown Atlantic gale.

It is here that King Edward VII and Queen Alexandra, while Prince and Princess of Wales, paid a visit and went underground, indeed under the sea bed. They wished to see for themselves the conditions experienced by the men of that era.

Today, there remain only the shells of the engine houses, in themselves, a memorial to those men.

THE WALK

❶ Leave the car park and turn left following the coastal path sign for Botallack. The track is wide and easy to follow. In about 1 mile pass a house. The track becomes 'made up'. You now approach Botallack Head. The Crown engine houses soon come into view. If you decide to venture down for a closer look, do beware of slippery paths.

❷ To continue the walk stay on the wide track bearing left and pause to visit the Old Count House for the mine. It is now managed by the National Trust and acts

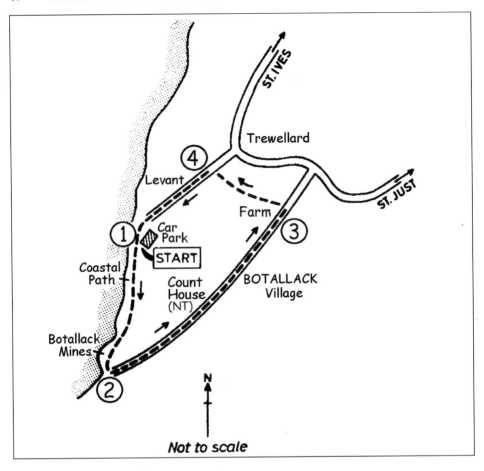

as an information centre for the area with displays of flora and fauna as well as mineral and mining history.

❸ You leave the coast path here bearing left past Manor Farm. Scenes from the *Poldark* TV series were shot in this location. Pass the track leading to the farm barns on your left and take the next track to the right of it. There was no waymark at the time of writing but a definitive footpath leads across farmland. It is well walked and has adequate stiles.

❹ Join a track which, in turn, joins the Levant road. Turn left for your car. However, a short stroll to the right will bring you into Trewellard village with its teashop and pubs.

FOOD and DRINK

In Trewellard, you will find the Trewellard Arms Hotel. Telephone: 01736 788634. The Field House Café, also in Trewellard is another suitable refreshment stop though it is only open from Easter to October.

ST JUST

Length : 6 miles

Getting there: St Just lies 7 miles from Penzance. Take the A3071 road out of Penzance and follow the signs all the way to St Just.	**Parking:** On reaching the town square turn left where in a few yards you will see a car park on the left.	**Map:** OS Explorer 102 (GR 373313).

The area around St Just was once the scene of tin and copper mining. There are many vivid reminders of the past to be seen in the tall engine houses which contained the engines to pump the water from the mines. Geevor Mine is situated a few miles along the road to Pendeen and visitors can see mining relics and present day methods of extracting the ore. It is also possible to go underground here and you can check opening times by phoning 01736 788662.

Just to the left of the village square is a grassed area of a Medieval Round, a site where miracle plays were performed and

Cape Cornwall

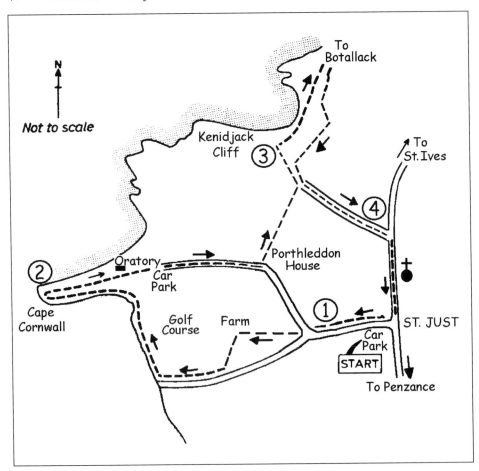

meetings took place; indeed, even today, it is the scene of folk festivals and the like.

Cape Cornwall is the only cape in England. If you climb up to the engine house – and who could resist the challenge? – you will be able to see the Longships lighthouse off Lands End and the Brisons rocks just to the left. Many a shipping disaster has occurred here. St Helens oratory was situated at the foot of the cape and outlines of the buildings are still visible today.

Do spare time to look in the church at St Just. You will see 5th-century wall paintings of Christ of the Trades and of St George and the Dragon and a pillar stone with the Chi-Rho monogram is an unusual feature in the churchyard.

THE WALK

❶ Walk back to the road and turn left. Continue past the school until you reach the cricket ground on your right. Opposite this is a lane and a footpath sign and stile.

You can use the lane but it is very narrow. The field paths offer more pleasant walking. Climb the stile and take the path to the farm. Still following the path, turn left across the field and join the lane. Turn right. Continue to the open space at Carn Gloose and join the coast path, turning right through a gateway. Carry on to Cape Cornwall.

❷ After exploring the Cape, turn right up the lane. Just as the road bears to the right, turn left below the wall of Porthleddon House. Continue along the valley side for nearly a mile until you reach Boscean Farm. Turn left down to a stream, over the bridge, then left again along the track to the summit of Kenidjack Cliff.

❸ Just before the quarry, turn right up a steep path to the summit. Continue along this high level path around the cliff top to Botallack Head. To continue the walk, after perhaps visiting the Crown Houses described in the previous walk, it is necessary to retrace the path back as far as the valley, known as the Tregaseal Valley. Turn left here and follow the track all the way to the road.

❹ On reaching the road, turn right, up a steep hill, back to the village and car park.

FOOD and DRINK

The Kings Arms in the Market Square is heartily recommended. Telephone: 01736 788545. There are also various cafés, bakers and other pubs in the town. During the summer you will also find refreshments available in the National Trust car park at Cape Cornwall.

SENNEN COVE AND LANDS END

Length : 4 miles

Getting there: Take the A30 from Penzance to Land's End. **Parking:** In the car park at	Land's End, for which a charge is made. Alternatively, park at Sennen Cove and start the walk from there.	**Map:** OS Explorer 102 (GR 342250).

Land's End, the most westerly point of England, has always been a magnet to draw the crowds, whether they be British or foreign. In Roman times both Diodoras and Ptolemy referred to Land's End as Bolerium, the seat of storms. There are, indeed, few days in the year when all is calm at Land's End.

Sadly, Land's End is suffering from the ravages of time. The many pilgrims to this spot have left their mark and conservationists are using their skills to find a solution to the problem. A successful visitor centre and hotel now form a base for the many people who visit this special place. A large car parking area has been established and there is a charge for the use of this and the facilities within the centre. However, should you wish to walk this route in reverse of the directions given here, starting from Sennen Cove and approaching Land's End from the coastal footpath, no charge is made, unless you wish to visit the museum and displays available in the centre. There are various car parks in Sennen.

Sennen Cove is guarded by the headland of Pedn-men-Dhu and, more southerly, by

Mayon Cliff. The village is delightful. Within the sweep of Whitesand Bay it is a surfer's paradise – and the lifeboat which serves this treacherous area is housed here. An unusual round building above the beach is the capstan house which used to house the machinery, turned by donkeys, for pulling the boats up the steeply shelved beach.

Sennen village, on the A30, is situated above the cove. The church, dedicated in 1441, owes its origin to St Senan, a priest who reached Cornwall from Ireland in about the 6th century. Not far from the church is the Table-Mên, a block of granite 7 ft 10 in long. Legend has it that at this stone seven Saxon kings dined after defeating the Danes at Villan Druacher about AD 600. Merlin prophesied that peace will return to the earth when seven kings dine here again.

THE WALK

❶ Leave the car and walk away from the hotel towards the First and Last House taking the most convenient path away from the headland to join up with the coastal footpath. This is well-defined

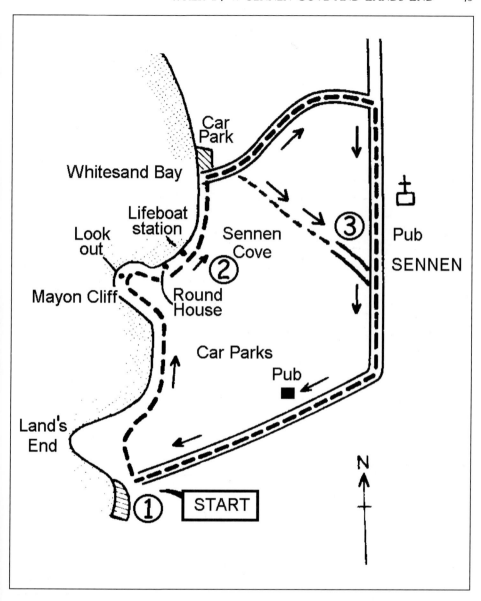

and easy to follow although there are some boggy places. The Isles of Scilly which lie 28 miles off Land's End can often be seen from here. Mayon Cliff ahead has a coastguard look-out post on the Pedn-men-Dhu headland.

❷ The path descends steeply into the village of Sennen Cove and enters it through a car park. The round house is

Breakwater at Sennen Cove

situated here. Walk across the car park and along the village street, passing the lifeboat house on the left. Here the full beauty of Whitesand Bay delights the eye with Cape Cornwall in the distance. Just to the south of the Cape lie the Brison Rocks, the scene of many a tragic shipwreck in days of sail.

FOOD and DRINK

There are refreshments facilities at Land's End and various cafés and takeaways in Sennen village. The Old Success Inn, Sennen is a welcoming 17th-century pub and heartily recommended. Telephone: 01736 871232.

For the botanist, a detour along the beach to the lifeguard hut should prove worthwhile. Here may be seen, among other flora, the lovely sea holly. Explore the village and return to the round house. Walk up Daisy Chain Lane just opposite. When this short lane ends continue on the footpath.

❸   On reaching a road, Marias Lane, turn right. At the next junction, cross over and turn right using the footpath. At the T-junction turn right. There is a footpath back to Land's End which joins the Cornish Way for the last few hundred yards.

LAMORNA AND TATER-DU LIGHTHOUSE

Length : 5 miles

Getting there: From Penzance, take the coast road to Newlyn and then the B3315 for Lamorna, turning left after about 6 miles (signposted).	**Parking:** In the car park at Lamorna Cove.	**Map:** OS Explorer 102 (GR 451241).

This rugged stretch of coastline has a variety of features which are especially interesting. You can see a prehistoric stone circle, standing stones and an ancient burial site. At the start of the walk you will pass the 'Silent Cross of Lamorna'. This granite cross stands below a vast pile of lichen covered rocks. It is about 5 feet high and has no name, no inscription and bears no date. It is set on a levelled rock and stands there, a silent tribute to something or someone.

The path is easily followed, passing Tater-Du lighthouse which is operated in conjunction with Lizard Light. The village of Lamorna has always been an artists' paradise and still is today. This is a

---

FOOD and DRINK

There is a café at the cove which is open all year and nearby is the Lamorna Wink, a friendly pub which is open all day throughout the year. Telephone: 01736 733566.

---

memorable walk, with a chance to experience the charm of this remote area of the Duchy.

THE WALK

❶ Take the path to the right of the car park and follow this for a few hundred yards. You may have to clamber over a few fallen boulders. Very soon the 'Silent Cross' comes into sight. After passing the cross continue to follow the coast path along Tregurrow Cliff.

❷ There is a stile at the top, then a steep downhill before ascending again to pass through old bulb fields. The path is easy to follow and comes out onto a track leading to the lighthouse.

❸ Up the track behind the lighthouse a gate is reached. The coastal path continues to the left onwards towards Land's End. Our route takes the wide track past a house on the right which used to be a row of

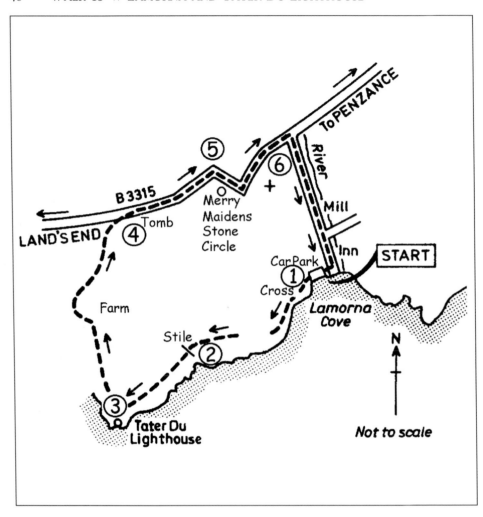

coastguard cottages. Continue along the lane towards Boscowen Rose Farm. Passing the farm to the right the lane bears left and then right as it wends its way to join the B3315 at a T-junction.

❹ Apart from a short footpath it is necessary to use the roads back to Lamorna from this point. Turn right at the T-junction where, almost immediately

on the right is the Megalithic chamber tomb. This came to light during the road widenings and it is to the County Council's credit that a good job was made of protecting it.

❺ The next field on the right past the tomb is the location for the best known of the Cornish stone circles, known as the 'Merry Maidens', so-called because they are

Lamorna Cove

said to have been turned to stone for dancing on a Sunday. The two large stones at the top of the hill are said to be the two pipers who were playing for them. There is a footpath past the circle to rejoin the road. Continue along the road until the next right turn.

❻   This is the road used earlier during the car journey to the start of the walk. As you walk down this lovely valley now is the time to appreciate the flowers, shrubs and trees. Pass, or stop at, the Lamorna Wink public house and enjoy the delights of this special part of Cornwall.

MOUSEHOLE

Length : 5¹/₂ miles

Getting there: Take the coast road from Penzance signposted to Newlyn and Mousehole. Pass through Newlyn where the road winds its way through narrow streets and past Penlee Quarry where road stone is extracted. The next village is Mousehole.

Parking: In the large council car park on the left just before entering Mousehole.

Map: OS Explorer 102 (GR 470264).

Penzance harbour

This walk includes two of the most picturesque villages in west Cornwall. Mousehole is a typical fishing village with narrow winding streets and old houses in little alleyways. The colourwashed cottages are a delight and the Ship Inn a typical fisherman's hostelry. This village was the home of Dolly Pentreath, the lady reputed to be the last person to use the Cornish language as her native tongue. The remains of her cottage can still be seen. There are many artists' studios and other craft workshops. Take a look at the Bird Sanctuary as you pass it to join the coast path.

Lamorna is unique. Nestling between huge rocky outcrops this tiny cluster of houses is a true Cornish gem. Visit the Old Mill with its green tapestry of huge plants and a craft shop offering local goods. The water-wheel has long since ceased its busy life but the stream which fed it still meanders through this lovely place.

THE WALK

❶ Leave the car park by the exit in the right-hand corner. This leads to a path almost on the shore. Turn right towards the village and follow the path into another car park. Cross this into the main street.

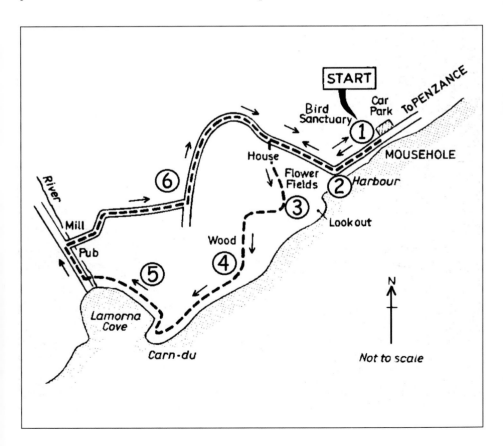

❷   Take the road that follows the harbour wall and bear right making for the Methodist Chapel at the bottom of the hill leading to the bird sanctuary. At the top of the hill the road levels out. Pass two very pretty cottages and take the sign on the left marked 'Footpath Lamorna'.

❸   This is the old coastguard's path and still leads to a look-out post. The path runs through old flower fields where early crops used to catch the London market. Great, flat, granite slabs flank the shore making an ideal spot for sunbathing or fishing.

❹   After about a mile the path enters a wood, quite unusual on a coastal footpath. On emerging, climb the stile and continue for a short distance, then round a headland. The path is near the edge in places here and some boulders have to be climbed over. On turning the corner Lamorna comes into sight. Although it may only look a few minutes' away there is, in fact, still some quite hard walking to be done. The boulders are many and care should be taken.

❺   The entrance to the village is past a disused granite quarry. Stone from this was used to build the Thames embankment in London. On reaching the car park, turn right up a rather steep road which leads to the village. The old inn known as 'The Wink' is on the right and immediately past it is a turn to the right. Here you will find the mill with its water plants of vast proportions.

❻   There is a footpath back to Mousehole along the roads and over the fields, or you can just follow this road up the hill from the mill. It is well signposted back to Mousehole and still remains a quietly pretty lane. Personally, I think to retrace one's steps along the coast path is much the best. All the things you missed on the outward trek can be appreciated on the way back.

FOOD and DRINK

The Ship Inn in Mousehole is a traditional Cornish pub overlooking the harbour. It is open all day throughout the year. Telephone: 01736 731234.

ST MICHAEL'S MOUNT AND PENZANCE

Length : 6 miles

Getting there: From Penzance, take the A30 road to Redruth. Turn right to Marazion and at the T-junction, turn left.	Parking: There are numerous car parks along the roadside before you reach the village of Marazion.	Map: OS Explorer 102 (GR 513310).

A jaunt around St Michael's Mount and a visit to Penzance are on offer with this delightful walk.

If the tide is right you can walk to the Mount along the causeway whose stones were laid by the order of Benedictine monks who possessed the island for 370 years. It was the men from this order of

St Michael's Mount

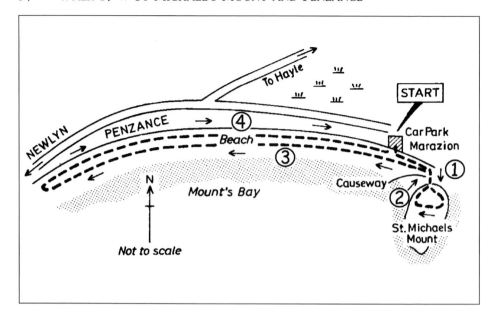

monks who built the first harbour at Mousehole in 1392. In 1414 when many monasteries were being suppressed, St Michael's was granted to a group of nuns from Isleworth and in 1537, after Henry VIII passed a law to regain the mount, it was held by Humphrey Arundell of Lanherne. That was until he was hanged for his part in the uprising against the new Prayer Book. (Cornwall held to the Roman Catholic faith until the very last.) The Mount was later sold by James I and it then came into Bassett hands and to the St Aubyn family who are the present inhabitants, although the greater part of the Mount is administered by the National Trust. St Michael's Mount and Mont St Michel in Normandy are closely allied and St Michael himself is said to have appeared at both places.

After reaching the island, take a good look at all the delightful little cottages facing across the harbour and then walk up the steep path to the castle and church. Ancient writings tell us that trees surrounded the rock at one time.

Penzance beckons you after leaving the Mount. This truly Cornish town with so many interesting features deserves time to explore its fascinating backways and, of course, the harbour is a 'must'. Penzance is the only Cornish resort with a promenade, and seats and gardens line this pleasant area.

If you have time, you could extend your walk by continuing along the promenade to Newlyn, home of the Cornish fishing fleet.

THE WALK

Note: A check with the tide chart must be made before crossing the causeway to St Michael's Mount as it is only accessible at certain states of the tide. For information, particularly in the winter when the ferry may not be operating, contact the Estate Office in Penzance, telephone: 01736 710507.

❶ Assuming that the tide is low and the causeway can be used, walk across the beach for a short distance before joining the causeway to the Mount. After exploring the area around the harbour, walk up the steep path to the castle and church.

❷ After you have explored the island, leave it by ferry or causeway, and walk across the beach towards Penzance. There is a path along the top of the sea wall but, tide permitting, the beach is the best as it avoids necessary detours for streams. This beach may well yield some good specimens of jasper and agate for the collector.

FOOD and DRINK

There is a café on St Michael's Mount which is open during the summer months. Otherwise the Station House, Longrock, just off the coastal path, offers food and drink all day. Telephone: 01736 350459. Needless to say, refreshments are also available at various pubs and cafés in both Penzance and Marazion.

❸ Follow the path to the gardens which run alongside the main road. It is then footpath all the way into Penzance, about half a mile. You will, no doubt spend time here and, perhaps, take the promenade walk into Newlyn.

❹ The walk back is necessarily over the same ground but with St Michael's Mount as the distant lure the way seems very short.

PENROSE WOODS AND LOE POOL

Length : 7 miles

Getting there: From Falmouth, take the A394 road for Helston. Use the bypass signed Penzance and Lizard. At the first roundabout past Tesco turn right, taking the Penzance sign. Follow these	signs around the town. At a T-junction/roundabout take the Penzance sign but almost immediately turn left with a leisure park area on your right.	Parking: At the leisure park area. Map: OS Explorer 8 (GR 658272).

This route begins with pleasant easy walking on a wide and firm track sheltered by trees and bushes. It then continues on the coast path where Mounts Bay in all its splendour lies in front and the sands beneath the cliffs stretch for about three miles. It was just here that Henry Trengrouse watched a ship sink and saw the drowning of hundreds of men, from which sorry sight came his inspiration for the rocket apparatus (warning flares) still in use today.

You will walk alongside the Loe Bar which is really the estuary of the river Cober. The river's entrance to the sea was blocked when a sand bar was thrown up during a severe storm in the Middle Ages causing severe flooding in Helston. There is now an underground culvert for the water to pass through but for many years the bar had to be broken manually to release the water.

The bar is owned by the National Trust and is a place frequented by collectors of pebbles and stones which have already had the benefit here of several weeks' polishing by the tumbling action of the sea. The

massive waves rolling in can make this a dangerous place for bathing and there are not many days of the year when the red flag is not flying.

As you make your way across the bar, look out for sea holly and the rare horned poppy which have their habitat here. This walk of wide variety is close to the interesting town of Helston, home of the Furry Dance which takes place, annually, on 8th May. The dances begin at 7 am and continue throughout the day at intervals. The midday dances are the most spectacular. The ladies wear long dresses and picture hats and the men top hats and tails. The dance takes them in and out of houses and shops accompanied by the local band and the town is decorated with spring flowers, particularly lily of the valley.

THE WALK

❶ Turn right out of the car park. Walk for about 200 yards and cross over at the entrance to the woods. There is a gate marking the entrance to the Penrose woods. You should look for a hide here on the left after passing a cottage on your

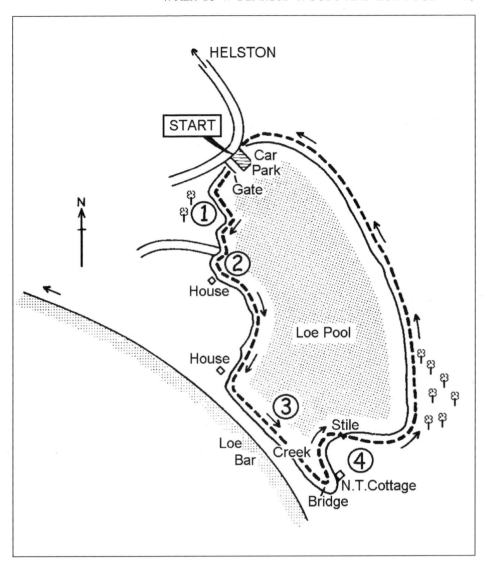

right. It overlooks the pool where you can expect to see coot, great black-backed gulls as well as blackheaded gulls, terns and herons.

❷   Return to the main track. You will soon see a large house on the right. Just

before you reach this there is a turn to the left signposted 'Loe Bar'. Take this path, uphill. The track eventually emerges from the woods and out onto the coastal footpath. Mounts Bay lies ahead.

❸   After joining the coast path, turn left

Loe Bar

and cross the bar which can be heavy going in the shingle. This is the habitat of the sea holly and horned poppy. When the trudge across the bar has been accomplished take the path skirting the pool. This can be muddy and uneven at times, quite different from the well-kept drive on the other side. Follow the path all the way round the pool, going inland. Cross the stream by a small wooden bridge and turn left, passing a National Trust holiday cottage on the right – a delightful spot for a get-away-from-it-all holiday.

❹   Continue along the track past the cottage until a granite stile in the left-hand wall comes into sight. Climb over the stile and skirt the field alongside the pool. The path goes right round the field and into the Denbigh woods. The path is now easy and pretty with woodland plants and birds. It passes through the Loe valley and emerges through a recreation field on to the road and so back to the car park.

FOOD and DRINK

The Blue Anchor Inn at Helston is a good stop. Their own beer 'SPINGO' is brewed on the premises. Telephone: 01326 562821.

LIZARD HEAD

Length : 5 miles

Getting there: From Helston, take the A3083 road passing through Culdrose Naval Air Station to reach Lizard.	**Parking:** There is a large free car park in the centre of the village.	**Map:** OS Explorer 8 (GR 703126).

The Lizard area of Cornwall is unusual not only in its geology but in its flora, for in the district above Kynance Cove the rare Cornish heath (Erica Vagans) can be found. The area is protected, in parts, by the Cornish Naturalists Trust and here may also be found the early purple orchid, harebells and bloody cranesbill. The pretty blue squill and the lovely thrift combine to make a pleasing picture in the spring. As for the bird life, you can see cuckoos, ravens, a buzzard or two and kestrels, while redwings and fieldfares may be observed in the winter. Snipe and mallard occasionally

The Lizard lifeboat house

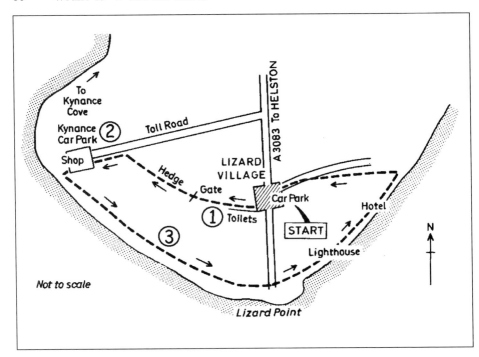

rest on the wet ditches. Very rarely, in winter, the short-eared owl, hen harrier and merlin may be sighted, too.

Much of Lizard village is devoted to the working of the serpentine rock for which this part of Cornwall is famous. Their busy craftsmen in their workshop *cum* salerooms are usually surrounded by interested tourists. The lighthouses, ashtrays and other ornaments they produce are beautifully polished to bring out the colours of red, green and black of the serpentine.

FOOD and DRINK

The Top House in Lizard village is open all year. Telephone: 01326 290456. During the summer, the café at Kynance Cove is a convenient place for a welcome drink.

During this walk, improbable as it may seem, you will walk along a Cornish hedge. This is a double stone wall filled with soil and turfed over making it perfectly possible for a path along the top. You will also have the opportunity to visit Kynance Cove. While most will enjoy the view from the coastal path, some of the more energetic may like to descend the steep path to the beach, particularly if the tide is low, for then the beautifully coloured rocks will be fully exposed and the caves accessible. **Watch the tide if crossing to the islands as it comes in very quickly here.** The detour from the path down into the cove is not really necessary, however, as the view from the clifftop is spectacular. You will probably see shag and cormorant diving for food while the gulls scream overhead.

At Lizard Point notice the succulent called mesembrianthemum with its big yellow or purple flowers cascading down the cliffs. The old Lizard lifeboat house still remains on the beach below the Point. It has not been used since the building of a new one at Kilcobben Cove in 1961. It is interesting to note that one-third of the world's shipping passes Lizard Point so one can see how important a lighthouse and lifeboat are on this dangerous rocky shore.

THE WALK

❶ Walk along the road past the public toilets and a small craft shop. Take the right-hand track signed to Kynance Cove. Just before a metal gate, with a white shed on the left, bear left along a footpath and up some steps onto a Cornish hedge. Cross a field and join a metalled road leading to the Kynance Cove parking area. Turn left at the road, into the car park and, passing behind a shop, join the coastal footpath.

❷ This is where you can detour into the cove. To continue the walk, take the path behind the shop away from the cove and follow it as it wends its way towards Lizard Point. It is wide here and the walking is easy on the springy turf. On reaching the Point and for a shorter walk, follow the road back up to Lizard village. For the full walk continue on the coast path passing the lighthouse.

❸ The path now becomes steeper and narrower as it passes Bass Point and Housel Bay. The bay is renowned for its geological features such as hornblend and gneiss. After crossing a narrow bridge the path ascends steeply. Keep right at the fork, passing in front of Housel Bay Hotel. Just past the hotel turn left at a sign marked 'Lizard village', onto a hard track which joins a metalled road into the centre of the village opposite the car park.

KENNACK SANDS AND CADGWITH

Length : 5 miles

Getting there: Take the A3083 road from Helston signed for the Lizard. After passing through Culdrose Naval Air Station there is a roundabout. Turn left here signed 'St Keverne, Mawgan and Goonhilly Downs'. Take this road, the B3293 and follow the signs for St Keverne for about 5 miles. Shortly after passing Goonhilly Satellite Station, turn right, signed Kennack.

Parking: There is a large car park at the beach (fee payable).

Map: OS Explorer 8 (GR 739168).

This walk begins on the coastal footpath, goes inland for about two miles through a delightful hamlet and then through the village of Cadgwith and back to the coastal path for the return journey. Some of the paths can be rather muddy and there is one steep climb; otherwise the going is easy and the scenery beautiful. Part of the walk is on a nature trail and as this part of the Lizard is noted for its flora the botanist should be in his element. The village of Cadgwith is much used for Cornish publicity literature and when one looks down on the delightful thatched and colourwashed cottages, with the little harbour nestling in the centre, one can appreciate why.

You will also see the geological feature known as the Devil's Frying Pan. This spectacular sight was created when the back of a giant sea cave collapsed about a century ago. You will also pass a small building known as the huer's hut. It is here that, as in Newquay, a huer would be stationed to watch for the shoals of pilchards which arrived between August and November.

THE WALK

❶ Walk back up the hill, keeping to the road. Do not attempt to walk along the coast. Just past the lay-by halfway up the hill is a footpath on the left (the sign was broken when I walked it). This path joins the coast path. There are good views from here across the sands to Black Head. The rocks below are formed of bastite and serpentine and the mineral asbestos can also be found here.

❷ Continue to follow the coast path to reach a field and caravan site. Walk through this field, then up an incline and over a rather awkward stile. Next comes a steep descent and the narrow path widens out into a rough track. On the left, at the bottom, are some buildings. These were an old serpentine works and they have to some extent been preserved. It is easy to see what

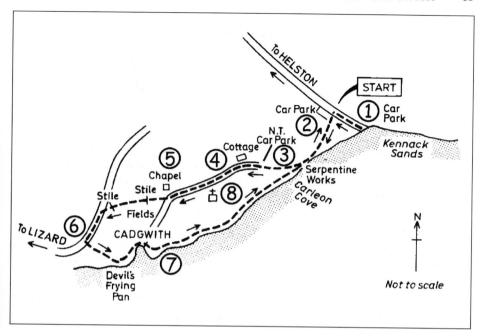

a considerable area they occupied at one time. There are the remains of a kiln here, too. This is where the Poltescoe river enters the sea at Carleon Cove.

❸ Cross the wooden bridge and turn right up some steps, away from the coast. The walk goes inland now and there is a National Trust sign marked 'Poltescoe' here. Notice the bamboo and other interesting plants on the side of the path for this is part of the nature trail which continues through a lightly wooded area, past some houses, until the path widens out into a drive. Walk on and over a bridge to the road with a National Trust car park on the right. Turn left and walk up the road, turning left at the fork opposite a cottage.

❹ Another bridge over the Poltescoe river has now to be crossed and an interesting feature is the old boundary marking carved in the granite slab on the left of the bridge. Just halfway across will be seen a line, on which one side is marked 'Gade' and on the other 'Ruan' for this line marks the boundary of two parishes. Note the water-wheel beside the river. Continue up the road past a cottage or two and then into the village of Ruan Minor entering the village by the school. Turn left, past the school, then turn right at a sign for Cadgwith. The church is nearby and is worth a visit. It was restored in 1854 but has a 13th-century font and piscina. There are serpentine blocks in the walls.

❺ Walk through the village towards Cadgwith for a few yards and look for the Methodist chapel on the right. Leave the road and take the path to the left of the

Cadgwith

chapel. Cross a field and then climb a granite slab stile. Notice the holy well on the left. Pass over another granite slab stile and go downhill to the road. Turn left and follow the road to the junction.

❻ Ignore the first left turn signed 'Cadgwith' but take the next unsigned road a few yards further on. This is a narrow lane. As it is about to wind round to the right, at a sign marked 'The Lizard', leave the road and turn left. There is a sign here for the Devil's Frying Pan. Bear right through a gateway with a sign saying 'Ingleswidden'. At the next bend keep left. In a short distance look for a sign on the right for Ingleswidden. There is an open space here and some holiday cottages. In the far right corner of the open space is a stile. Go over this and

onto the coastal path. Almost immediately you can look down into the Devil's Frying Pan. Take care, though, for the cliff is very steep here.

❼ Retrace the path back to the open space and rejoin the original track. Turn right downhill past some cottages, indeed through the garden of one, which is the right of way. From here, some of the best views of Cadgwith may be had. Join the road and turn right down the hill to the beach. The beach is stoney and the fishing boats are drawn up close to the road. Lobster and crab pots are stacked and nets are spread out to dry. There is also a shop here where shellfish can be purchased. This is Cornwall at its best, quite unspoiled.

❽   Continue on through the village and start to ascend the hill. Just round the bend is a footpath sign pointing to the right. Pass between two rows of cottages, up the wide track overlooking the beach. At a fork keep to the right. This is where the huer's hut will be found. Bear to the left and keep to the coastal path walking over Kildown Point and Enys Head. There are one or two step stiles to negotiate. At an open space keep to the left around the gorse bushes. At the next fork keep to the right then over another stile. Stay on the track nearest the sea and then go downhill to the serpentine works again. The walk now retraces the outward journey along the coastal footpath back to Kennack Sands.

FOOD and DRINK

Kennack has an interesting pottery/tea shop which is open all year round. The Cadgwith Cove Inn in Cadgwith is a traditional Cornish pub offering good food and is open all day during the summer. Telephone: 01326 290513.

HELFORD AND MANACCAN

Length : 5¹/₂ miles

Getting there: Take the A3083 from Helston signposted to 'The Lizard'. On reaching Culdrose Naval Air Station continue to the	roundabout. Turn left following the St Keverne sign on the B3293. Turn left for Helford and Manaccan.	**Parking:** In the car park overlooking the river. **Map:** OS Explorer 8 (GR 760260).

This walk incorporates both coastal and inland paths, a 'must' for those exploring the Lizard area. It is particularly beautiful in the spring as parts are wooded and wild flowers grow in profusion. Daphne Du Maurier's novel *Frenchman's Creek* was written in the area and one can imagine many of its scenes when walking this path.

You will have the opportunity to visit two churches: one at St Anthony and the other at Manaccan. While most churches in the area are built of local stone, St Anthony's church is built with stone from Normandy. Legend has it that, after being shipwrecked, a group of Norman sailors built the tower with stone brought from their own country as a thanksgiving for being saved from drowning on this shore. Note the ancient whipping post near the entrance. At Manaccan one may be surprised to see a fig tree growing out of the walls of the tower.

Helford village is a delight: totally unspoilt its pretty cottages line the water's edge as the boats lie at anchor below. A ferry operates between Helford and Helford Passage just across the water. Access is along a path which you join past the pub at the end of the village.

THE WALK

Note: Stout shoes or boots are necessary as parts of the woodland paths can be slippery.

❶ Take the path adjacent to the car park marked 'Coast Path'. A short walk through woodland ends in a tarmac lane. Turn right here and ascend the hill until you reach a gate on the left. This marks the entrance to Bosahan Woods, a public right of way through privately owned grounds. No dogs are allowed.

❷ The path now wends its way close to the shore in places, where numerous sea birds can be observed. Yachts and dinghies tack up and down the river. The path is clearly defined and crosses a small beach before emerging on to open fields. The view across Falmouth Bay is spectacular. Walk across the first field and over a stile then turn right in the next field passing close to some barns where there is a gate on to a road. Turn left and go downhill into the

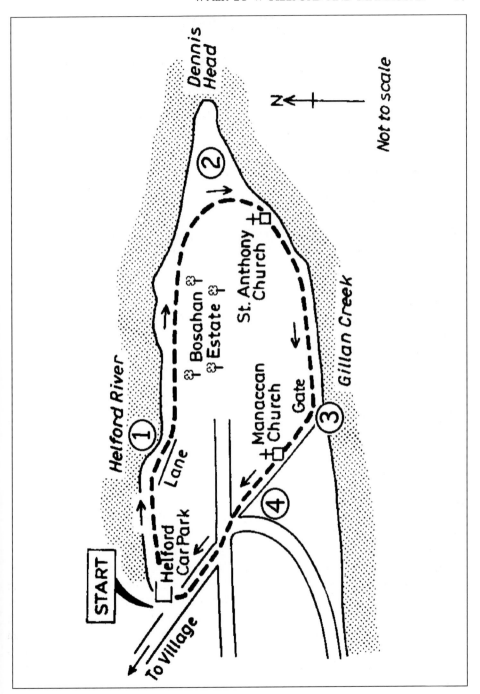

Helford

hamlet of St Anthony. This part of the river is called Gillan Creek.

❸   Boats are pulled up almost on the road here. The walk follows the lane bordering the creek, inland, for about 1 mile. Look out for a gate on the right with a footpath sign. Take this path, first leading through an area notable for its unusual plants and eventually coming to a lane at the back of Manaccan church.

❹   On leaving the church by the front gate, turn right, uphill, past the school. Continue on the road through the village to a crossroads. Take the Helford sign and

> **FOOD and DRINK**
>
> The Shipwrights Arms by the water's edge in Helford is a delightful spot to linger and enjoy some refreshments. It is open throughout the year. Telephone: 01326 231235.

walk downhill to the car park. Alternatively leave the road at the fourth gateway, with a footpath sign on your left. This goes a short distance along a wide track as if going to a farm. On reaching a gateway, turn right and follow the hedge on the left to a stile. Climb this and join the road not far from the car park.

ANTHONY HEAD

Length : 7 miles

Getting there: From St Austell, take the A390 to Truro. Turn left on the B3287 to Tregony, then take the A3078 for Gerrans and St Mawes. In Trewithian, turn left for Gerrans. Pass through the village and turn left to Anthony Head.

Parking: In the National Trust car park at Porth Farm on the right of the river.

Map: OS Explorer 105 (GR 868329).

This circuit, in the beautiful Roseland area of south Cornwall, offers the walker some of the most spectacular scenery in this part of the county. It offers views over the Percuil river to St Mawes and across the Carrick Roads to Pendennis Point and Falmouth and includes a coastal footpath beside the English Channel. In total, the walk is a good seven miles, with some uphill walking, but the paths are well-defined and the variety offered more than compensates for the strenuous nature of the route.

THE WALK

❶ To begin the walk leave the car park and turn left along the lane you have just driven along. In about 150 yards on the left

---

FOOD and DRINK

The Old Watch House at St Mawes is open all day from Easter to December and has a licensed restaurant. Telephone: 01326 270279. To the north at Philleigh is the delightful Roseland Inn which is open all year round. Telephone: 01326 580254.

---

and rather obscured by vegetation in the summer, is a track leading to a wooden bridge. Take this track, cross the bridge, turn right and follow the path alongside the creek. There is a National Trust direction sign here for Place Manor, which is part of the walk. Cross a stile out of the field. The path now wends its way, uphill, through a lightly wooded area. Keep to the right of the next field and on emerging from the wood notice a small white hut on the shore.

❷ The views across the river here are lovely. You will see oyster beds marked with tall sticks close to the shore. This part of the river teems with birdlife. After passing a hut, climb a stile and at a fork in the path keep to the right. Shortly after this you will find a very conveniently placed seat. Continue along this path, again through a small wood until reaching the sign marked 'Drawlers Plantation'. Go through the kissing-gate and in a short distance Place Manor comes into sight on the right. Go through the iron gate onto a road and turn left.

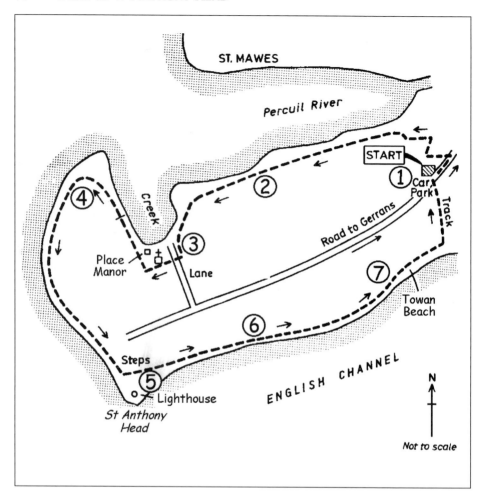

❸   Walk up the road for a few yards to a sign for Anthony Head. Take this path which goes through the churchyard where, in this peaceful spot, there is an abundance of wild flowers and hydrangeas. Turn left just opposite the church door and, after climbing a few steps, turn right. The walk continues along a wide, although rather muddy, track until a gate is reached. Climb the stile on the left, again signed 'Anthony Head'.

❹   At the top is a granite step stile over a wall. After negotiating this rather awkward stile turn left and follow the worn path, diagonally, downwards to your right. Make for the water's edge, passing through a gate in the electric fence. Follow the path along the top of the low cliff to a stile entering a small group of pine trees. After passing two coves on the right, cross over a bridge and up the other side turning to the right. Pass a gatepost bearing a National Trust

Looking towards St Mawes

boundary sign, adjacent to which are some steps leading onto a platform from which the view can be enjoyed. All kinds of sea birds can be seen. Proceed past a small white building on the right.

❺ Anthony Head lighthouse now lies ahead but is not normally open to the public. Just before reaching the lighthouse turn sharply left up a steep tarmac path. At a path junction proceed straight ahead up a number of steps. At the top, turn right, passing National Trust holiday cottages and some toilets. There are remains of wartime buildings hereabouts. The path makes its way through them. Continue to follow the coast and appreciate the magnificent scenery from the steep cliffs. The path runs near the edge in places and

there are some overhangs so caution is necessary.

❻ The coastal path is clearly defined and necessitates climbing one or two stiles. Halfway across a cultivated field are some steps leading to a beach and a path running through the centre of the field. Do not be tempted to take this path but walk straight on. The sandy bay on the right is known as Porthbeor.

❼ Pass through a gap in the hedge and so on to Killegerran Head, owned by the National Trust. Go through an iron gate, pass a white post and so on to Towan Beach. At the track leading up from the beach turn left and follow it to the road. Turn left to the lane and the car park is on the right.

RESTRONGUET CREEK

Length : 3 miles

Getting there: From Truro, take the A39 to Falmouth. Just after Perranarworthal turn left to Restronguet.

Parking: In the lane above the Pandora Inn at Restronguet.

Map: OS Explorer 105 (GR 815375).

This is not really a coastal walk but one that skirts the edge of Restronguet Creek, a creek of the river Fal. It is a sheltered walk, most suitable for a blustery or damp day. There are numerous creeks on the south coast and all provide interesting walking. Birdlife includes heron, dunlin, redshank and many species of gulls. The creek also boasts a most delightful inn, the Pandora. Truly a fisherman's haven, its thatched roof, old beams and fireplaces offer the traveller a welcome respite. A ferry used to operate from here to nearby Feock but now the jetty is used only for pleasure

Restronguet Creek

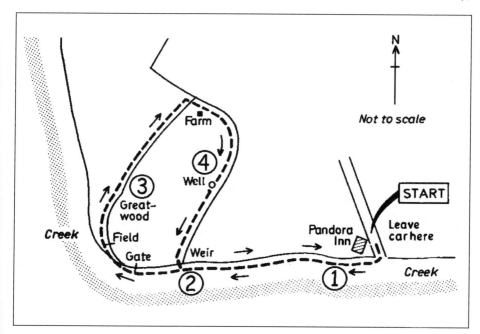

boats from Falmouth during the summer months.

THE WALK

❶ After leaving the car take the path which goes past the inn and rises slightly, passing some houses. Keep to the left at Dolphin Cottage and notice Restronguet Point on the opposite shore. Take the lower path at the next fork, passing more cottages. It is very sheltered here and fuchsia hedges may be seen flowering even in November. The path winds downhill and

---

FOOD and DRINK

The Pandora Inn is open all day during the summer months but closes in the afternoons from 2.30 pm to 6.30 pm October to Easter. Telephone: 01326 372678.

---

comes out on a beach at Restronguet Weir. Should the tide be high there is a gate and a path through a field just above the beach.

❷ The weir has now disappeared but this is a point of vehicular access to the shore. Cross the road and follow the sign marked 'Greatwood', continuing just above the creek. There is a wooden gate just after the sign and the right of way goes through this. At the next fork take the lower path which then goes through a rather muddy field before emerging onto a tarmac road at the hamlet of Greatwood. The old manor of that name stands here, very splendid, although now hosting numerous people in a modern flat complex. Walk at the right-hand side of the house, uphill, following the sign for Mylor Bridge.

❸ Continue on the road, shortly passing

The jetty alongside the pub at Restronguet

a signpost for Restronguet Barton. The next mile or so is road walking, but on a pleasant, leafy lane with views of the creek on the right and offering an abundance of flora with particularly good specimens of heart's tongue fern, hard fern and wall pennywort.

❹   At a crossroads take the sign marked 'Weir'. Walking downhill back towards the weir look for violets in the hedgerow, for they can be found here as early as January. As the road goes steeply downhill, notice two old wells on the right-hand side. These, I am told, were used by the local people for keeping their clotted cream cool during hot weather. Continue on this road to the weir and rejoin the original path, turning left back to the Pandora Inn.

COOMBE CREEK

Length : 4 miles

Getting there: Leave Truro on the bypass signed Redruth and Falmouth. Turn left at the roundabout for Falmouth. In about half a mile turn left at a sign for	Calenick. Drive through the village and at a T-junction turn left for Coombe. **Parking:** Along the lane or on the shore at Coombe	Creek. Be sure to keep above high water level. **Map:** OS Explorer 105 (GR 835410).

This walk is, strictly, not a coastal one but it does afford the walker pleasant creek views and sheltered walking. The path crosses farmland and overlooks the river Fal. The route is easily followed with substantial stiles and adequate footpath signs. The unspoiled creekside hamlet which is the starting point shelters many boats. Woodland reaches down to the shore in many places where waterfowl and waders make their nests. You will pass Old Kea church. The tower is 15th century

Coombe Creek

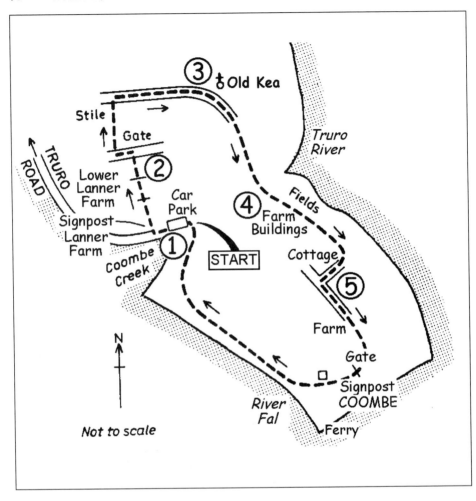

and is all that is left of the old parish church. The new one is several miles away at Kea. Do visit the little chapel. Generous gifts and bequests have made it possible to restore this building to the lovely place it is today.

THE WALK

❶ Take the path between two cottages signed to Lower Lanner Farm. Ascend the hill and cross the stile into the field.

Continue straight ahead over the top of the hill. Keep straight on, over another field to a gate and onto a lane. Turn left. In a few yards Lower Lanner Farm appears on the left.

❷ Almost immediately opposite, on the right, is a gate into a field. Go through this, skirt the field and at the other end climb over a stile onto a lane and turn right. In about a quarter of a mile the tower of Old

Kea church comes into view. Follow the road round to the right by a farm, to the churchyard.

❸ Pause here to look at the eerie old tower now falling into decay. Visit the little church close by. Continue down the lane to where it peters out. Pass the two houses on the left and take the footpath signed ahead.

❹ Follow this path to a gap in the hedge on the left. Step through this gap keeping to the right and near to the hedge. Make towards another gap where there are some farm buildings on the right. Walk through the gap and onto a track. Turn right, passing close to the farm buildings, through an iron gate. Continue on the track passing two cottages to reach a lane. Turn left here and climb the hill. Where the road abruptly ends join a track continuing to the left.

❺ Walk down this track and in a short distance on the right, is a gate with a signpost for Coombe. Follow this sign. At the end of the short track you will come to a renovated farmhouse. Keep to the right where you will find the path clearly marked leading you to a field skirting a wood. Look for a stile in the hedge on the left and climb over it into the wood. It is now an easy and very pleasant downhill walk through the woods back to Coombe and your car.

FOOD and DRINK

The nearest pub is the Punch Bowl and Ladle at Feock. Take the signs for Falmouth and at the Playing Place roundabout, turn left. The pub is a few yards further down on the left. Telephone: 01872 862237.

MEVAGISSEY

Length : 4 miles

Getting there: From St Austell, take the B3273 for Mevagissey and Pentewan. Stay on this road, passing the outskirts of Pentewan and make for Mevagissey.

Parking: There is a car park as you enter the village and another one at the harbour.

Map: OS Explorer 105 (GR 018449).

Mevagissey is a pretty little fishing village with winding streets, narrow, steep hills, a busy harbour and interesting shops. All these play their part in making this a pleasant place to while away a happy hour before beginning the walk. A local museum is situated alongside the harbour, a source of much information.

The walk is not too long but is steep in places and can be muddy over the fields in winter. On reaching Pentewan you will find there is still evidence of a yacht basin and locks. This one-time busy harbour boasted a tramway system which led out to the beach where ships were loaded with china clay and other minerals. The beach area is now completely silted up with sand and stone but many old buildings associated with the industry are still to be seen. Pentewan is a fascinating place for those interested in industrial archaeology. You will have lovely views across to Gribben Head with its day-mark. (A description of day-marks may be found in Walk 10.)

Here you are very close to the renowned Lost Gardens of Heligan which are signed en route from Pentewan to Mevagissey.

The Eden Project is also nearby and this is a good opportunity to visit this famous enterprise.

About 4 miles from Mevagissey is the little village of St Ewe. Off the beaten track and therefore often missed by visitors, it boasts a splendid old market cross adjacent to the church. The church is late 15th century, has a loft and a screen with coving. In the churchyard is a lovely camelia tree which is in full bloom in early February.

THE WALK

❶ From the car park make for the harbour. Almost immediately bear left following the coast path sign, up a steep incline in front of some cottages. The museum is just below. Continue up some steps and into a recreation field. Bear left across this field towards a gap in the hedge just below a row of houses. Go through the gap and along a fenced path. The path is well-defined. Cross over a granite step stile and cross the field diagonally towards the sea. There are two kissing-gates here and a wooden bridge.

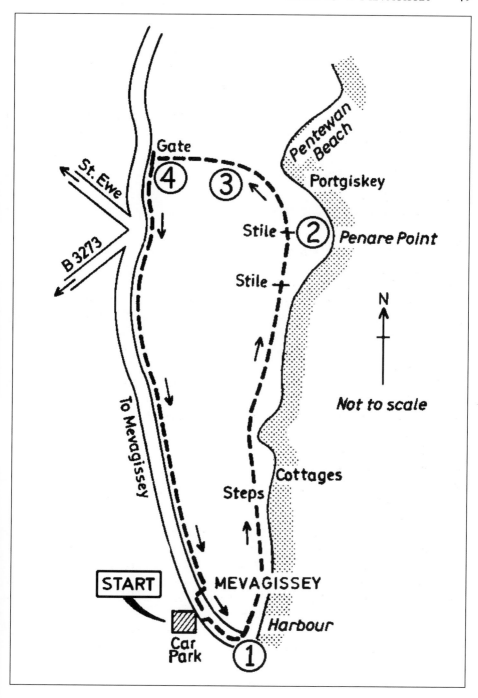

Mevagissey

❷ Cross over the bridge and keep left up a rather steep incline with lovely views to Gribbin Head. There is a stile at the top and, in a short distance, another stile. This leads into a field. Keep to the right and, on reaching the hedge, turn left. In a few yards is a stile on the right with a view overlooking Pentewan Sands.

❸ After crossing the stile, walk downhill over the next field, keeping to the right towards a stile at the bottom. Climb this stile and keeping to the right, climb to the top of the hill where there is a gate onto the path beside the road. You are overlooking Pentewan Sands Caravan Park.

❹ If you wish to visit Pentewan, then turn right here and walk down into the village. For Mevagissey, turn left onto a footpath beside the road. The distance back is about one and a half miles. The path hides itself from the road by passing in and out of screening bushes. As you near Mevagissey you will cross the cycle route to Heligan Gardens and so back to your car.

FOOD and DRINK

The Taste Buds Café, on the right as you enter Mevagissey, is open all year. Telephone: 01726 844347. In Pentewan, you will find a welcome at the Ship Inn. Telephone: 01726 842853.

FOWEY

Length : 4 miles

Getting there: Approaching Fowey on the A3082 from the north, you will reach a roundabout, just past a garage on the left. Take the third exit here. In about 500 yards look for a bus shelter on the right and a sharp right-hand turn into Lankelly Lane. Drive to a T-junction, Coombe Lane and turn left. This lane ends at a National Trust car park.

Parking: In the National Trust car park.

Map: OS Explorer 107 (GR 115518).

The area near Fowey is the location for this pleasant walk. There is a little road walking and some field walking. Two steep climbs have to be made along the coastal footpath but nothing that the average walker shouldn't be able to manage with ease. The view across the valley after entering the first field is towards Menabilly Woods but unfortunately the house of that name is obscured by trees. This was the home of Daphne Du Maurier and is now lived in by the Rashleigh family again who owned the property for centuries.

Fowey itself is a delightful, ancient town, named after the river beside which it is sited. It has a deep harbour, now used by ships exporting china clay and by yachts and pleasure craft. The winding, hilly streets with their small shops offering the visitor all kinds of local crafts, are a delight to browse in. The waterfront is an interesting place, too, with boatmen ready for a chat and many sea birds swooping among the boats. There is a museum and an aquarium to visit as well as a beautiful old church and other architecturally rare buildings.

The village of Polruan lies opposite, nestling into the steep cliff. The passenger ferry plies busily back and forth between the two places but travellers with cars must seek the Bodinnick ferry which crosses the river lower down.

THE WALK

❶ Turn left out of the car park onto a track. At the time of writing there was no footpath sign. Do not use the track signed to Coombe. Walk along this rather rough track. Just after it bears to the right there is a gate into fields. Cross two fields following a well-used path. You will be able to see the Menabilly estate from here and the day-mark on Gribbin Head.

❷ Continue to walk downhill where the scene will open out to give a lovely picture of Polridmouth Bay with a house and pool just above the beach. Continue to the bottom of the hill through a gate and turn left away from the house. The path now ascends through National Trust land into

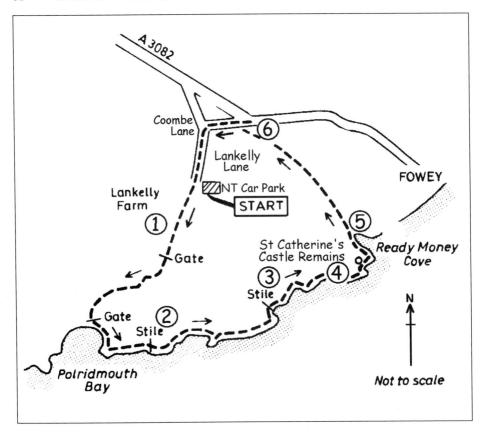

Lankelly Woods. Climb a stile at the top of the hill and turn right, following the path round the edge of the field on the sea side. This is the coastal footpath and easily followed.

❸ After a few steep ups and downs, cross a wooden bridge into Coombe Haven, a delightful sheltered cove. The views along this stretch of coast are across the Channel with Polperro in the far distance and nearby Polruan visible most of the way. The path eventually passes through an area known as Day Fields, given to the people of Fowey by Mr and Mrs Allday in 1951. Go through

the kissing-gate into the woods and keep straight on. Ignore all other paths and follow the wide track to the junction. Turn left here, though at this point, a detour can be made.

❹ Instead of turning left, turn right and the path will lead to St Catherine's Castle a fortification built by Henry VIII for defensive purposes. Notice a block house on either side of the river just below the castle. From these two towers a chain was suspended across the river in the days when Fowey was subjected to sacking from pirates. When this danger was imminent the chain

The view from St Catherine's Castle

was raised, thus preventing access into the estuary. Gun emplacements and cannon are still within the castle walls. Apart from its historical interest the place also offers the best vantage point for views down the river and of both Fowey and Polruan.

❺ To return to the walk. After turning left down the track, bear right at the

---

FOOD and DRINK

There is a variety of pubs and cafés in Fowey. Two to be recommended are the Lugger Hotel, telephone: 01726 833435, and the Galleon Inn, telephone: 01736 833014. Readymoney Cove also boasts a café which is open during the summer months.

---

bottom to a road above Readymoney Beach, so-called because of underwater artefacts beached here when divers have been exploring the many wrecks in the area. Pass by some pretty cottages and follow the road uphill. Almost at the top of the hill, turn left, opposite a pair of iron gates onto a wide track. Continue to follow this track for about half a mile until it ends at a lodge and gate.

❻ You are now back at Lankelly Lane. Turn into the lane. Take the first left turn and quite soon join a section of the Saints Way. This continues to a T-junction, Coombe Lane. Turn left here and so back to the car park.

WALK 27

POLKERRIS

Length : 5 miles

Getting there: From St Austell, take the A390 to Liskeard. After about 3 miles, turn right on the A3082 signposted to Fowey. Turn right off this road for Menabilly and Polkerris, and very shortly take a sharp right turn for Polkerris.

Parking: There is a car park halfway down the steep hill leading to the village.

Map: OS Explorer 107 (GR 095523).

This walk is in Daphne Du Maurier country, very close to the lovely house of Menabilly where the writer lived for a number of years. Polkerris is a delightful little village, nestling among the steep cliffs. Lush vegetation, quaint cottages, an old kiln and fish cellars: Polkerris has it all.

THE WALK

Note: The initial ascent from the village is steep and can be slippery after wet weather. Similarly the return route can be muddy in places so stout shoes are recommended.

❶ From the beach, walk a little way back past the cottages and turn right onto the coastal footpath. Pass the toilets and continue to follow the path, uphill, through the woods – a picture in springtime with primroses and bluebells. On reaching the field at the top, turn right and after a few yards climb over a stile. A view now opens out to show the expanse of St Austell Bay. The evidence of the china clay industry may seem rather jarring but it is essential to

the economy of the country as well as to Cornwall and is a small price to pay for the wealth it brings from natural resources. One quickly forgets the Port of Par by looking ahead at the sweep of the coastline towards Mevagissey.

❷ The path is easy to follow over the fields. It is recommended to take a sharp left turn uphill in the third field and then across the top and over a rather difficult stile on to Gribbin Head. There are signposts to 'The Gribbin' but the day-mark on the headland is as good a landmark as one could wish. (A description of day-marks can be found in Walk 10.) Take a look at this tall monument, erected as a guide for shipping during the 1880s. Look eastwards from here and notice Polruan in the distance. Further on is the coastline beyond Polperro.

❸ Follow the path away from the day-mark going downhill and round the little beach at the bottom. When the sign marked 'Polridmouth Beach' is reached,

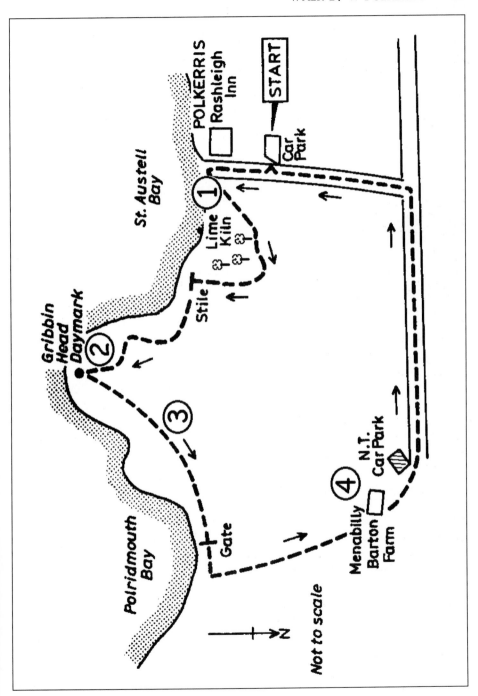

The Rashleigh Inn

take the left-hand path up the field away from the coast. However, before doing this, make a short detour by continuing along the coast path for a few yards. As it bends to the left a house set almost on the beach comes into view: the lake beside it and the cliff ahead give it one of the most picturesque settings possible.

❹   Back to the footpath – walk uphill through the field until it joins a track. This is where it can be quite muddy. Passing a farm on the left and into another field, keep to the farm track and through a gate onto a lane which leads back to join the road down into Polkerris again.

Just after joining the lane you will see the house of Menabilly to the right. The estate is now in the care of the Rashleigh family who owned the property for generations and now live in the house again.

FOOD and DRINK

The Rashleigh Inn occupies a superb position near the water's edge. There is an outside terrace overlooking the beach where you can relax and enjoy the good food and drink on offer. Telephone: 01726 813991.

CHEESEWRING, BODMIN MOOR

Length : 3 miles

Getting there: Take the Callington sign from Liskeard on the A390. In a few hundred yards turn left, signed St Cleer. On reaching this village and just before the church turn right, downhill to a T-junction. Turn left to Minions, turning right at the T-junction on the moor. There is also a sign for the Hurlers here.

Parking: Just before the village, on the left, is a parking space and a sign for the Hurlers pointing along a rough track. Leave the car here and start the walk along this track.

Map: OS Explorer 107 (GR 260712).

The Cheesewring

This is one of three moorland walks included in this book. The archaeological and geographical interest provided makes it one of the best short walks in the Bodmin Moor area. The terrain is a little rough in places and some climbing has to be done to the top of the tor. You will, almost immediately, see stone circles to the right of the track. A short descriptive plaque gives their date and possible use. This part of the moor abounds with evidence of very early habitation followed by the quarrying and mining activities of later dates. The engine houses, now mellowed and often surprisingly beautiful, are dominated by the Cheesewring, or Stowes Hill (1,249 ft) with its south slope scarred by the Cheesewring

quarry last worked in the 1950s. There are numerous paths leading to the Cheesewring, so called because of its structure of flat rocks of granite, naturally formed, piled one upon another. Those at the base are smaller than those at the top and the overall appearance is of a vast mushroom 24 ft high. The views from here, extending over both Devon and Cornwall, are truly magnificent.

An interesting place to look out for, before the final climb to the top, is a cave-like structure with some engraved granite blocks around it. The name, 'D.Gumb' is carved on one. Mr Gumb, his wife and 13 children are said to have lived in a cave here. He was a mathematician and

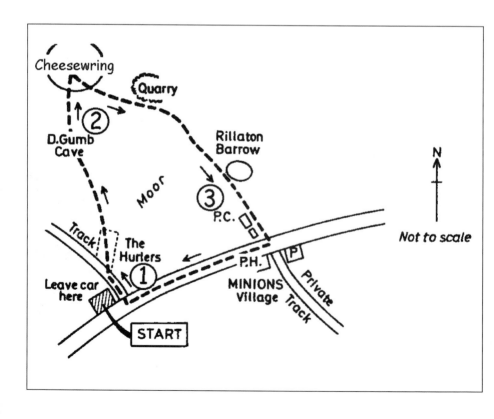

astronomer. Markings on other rocks show evidence of his pursuit of these subjects.

A short detour towards the end of the walk will take you to the Rillaton Barrow in which the famous gold cup of that name, dating from 1500 BC and now in the British Museum was found. You can see a short distance into the barrow through the gap around the entrance stone.

THE WALK

❶ Follow the track, visiting the Hurlers en route and take any of the various paths leading up to the Cheesewring, all very well trodden. Bear to the right as you start the last climb to see Daniel Gumb's cave.

❷ You will, I am sure, want to spend time walking around the Cheesewring. Descend

FOOD and DRINK

The Cheesewring Hotel in Minions retains all the character of a moorland inn and is open all year. Telephone: 01579 362321.

from the hill keeping to the path around the fenced edge of the quarry. On reaching a wide track – which was the tramway track into the quarry at one time – turn right. Just past some fenced mine shafts, bear right, diagonally, across the moor towards the Rillaton barrow, distinctive on the highest point in that area.

❸ From here, walk back to rejoin the track, turn right and follow it to where it joins the road. Turn right and make your way into Minions village and your car.

BODMIN MOOR, BROWN WILLY AND ROUGH TOR

Length : 4¹/₂ miles

Getting there: Leave Camelford by the A39, travelling north. Turn first right into a narrow lane and follow the sign for Rough Tor.

Parking: There is a spacious car park at the end of the road to Rough Tor.

Map: OS Explorer 109 (GR 138819).

This is rather a tough moorland walk which includes climbing the two highest tors in Cornwall. It is advisable to choose a clear day, for the mist comes down quickly in the high places; a very windy day should be avoided, too.

The first tor to be climbed is Rough Tor which is owned by the National Trust and

On Rough Tor

is the site of a memorial to the Wessex Regiment, 1,311 ft above sea level. There are numerous hut circles on the lower slopes of this tor and an old clapper bridge spans the stream crossing the approach track. The second is Brown Willy, 1,375 ft above sea level and giving views across the moorland to the A30 road at Jamaica Inn and Dartmoor to the north. Much can, and indeed has, been written about Bodmin Moor. All of it makes interesting reading but it is sufficient for me to say that this walk is a useful initiation into hill walking and, while it is not too long, it *is* rather strenuous.

THE WALK

Note: As already stated, choose a clear day, without a strong wind, for this outing.

❶   After leaving the car, walk down to the stream and the clapper bridge crossing it. Cross the bridge and follow the track up the slope ahead. It is shorter in distance to approach the summit by bearing to the

right and ascending the second half at the steepest angle, but for the easier, if longer, route I suggest that the track up the grassy slope be followed, to the left of the tor.

❷   On reaching the top of the lower slope, turn right and walk across to the massive boulders perched one above the other on the peak. This is not absolutely necessary but I feel that having come so far it is rewarding to complete the climb to the top where the Wessex Regiment memorial may be seen. The rocks are granite and are part of the intrusion of igneous rocks rising through the slates from Dartmoor out to the Isles of Scilly. This is a site much favoured by geological study groups as well as by climbing parties.

❸   After pausing for a while to take in the view and pick out various landmarks, walk down the other side of the tor, keeping to the left. There are boulders to contend with but it is easy enough to pick a way

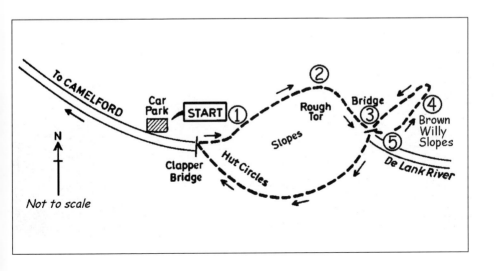

through. Brown Willy rises ahead and it is necessary to cross the De Lank river between the two tors. You will see a bridge in the valley and a gate through the fence. Cross the bridge, where it is rather muddy at most times of the year, and start the climb, which is gentle to begin with, up Brown Willy.

❹ Follow the track, well-defined, leaving a shepherd's derelict cottage on the right, where moorland ponies are often found sheltering between the two ridges. As the track bends away to the left, leave it and make your own way – there are numerous paths – up to the summit. The last few feet up to the cairn and trig point are steep. Here the wind blows, whatever the weather. The moors stretch ahead and traffic can be seen moving along the A30 at Jamaica Inn in the distance. In the marsh below rises the river Fowey. This area is known as the Fowey Downs.

FOOD and DRINK

Tiffins Tearooms in Camelford are open all year round though not Sunday. Telephone: 01840 213882. The Masons Arms is also a good stop for refreshments. Telephone: 01840 213309.

❺ For the return, descend from Brown Willy by the most convenient route, and make for the bridge again. Cross over this but do not climb over Rough Tor. Instead, turn left alongside a wall for a short distance then strike diagonally across the lower slopes towards the foot of the tor. It is uncomfortable to walk too close to the base, as it is so rocky. Keep bearing to the right, round the hill, and when the car park comes into sight again look out for the prehistoric hut circles which can be clearly seen, particularly when the grass is short. Join up with the original track and cross the clapper bridge again into the car park.

MADRON MOOR

Length : 4 miles

Getting there: Leave Penzance by crossing the bypass and taking the signs for Madron. After passing through the village, continue on this road over the moor until you reach a layby on the right and a sign for the Men an Tol.

Parking: In the layby as mentioned above.

Map: OS Explorer 102 (GR 418343).

Madron Moor is one of the granite outcrops running down the centre of Cornwall and out under the sea to the Isles of Scilly. It is from the contact with the country rock of slate that the mineralisation occurred. There is, as a result, evidence of extensive tin mining in this area. Compared with Dartmoor, or even Bodmin Moor, Madron is comparatively small in size but it is rich in archaeological remains. Here we find the greatest number of ancient burial grounds, old crosses, stone circles and standing stones. The burial sites range from barrows of Bronze Age origin to

The ancient monument of Men an Tol

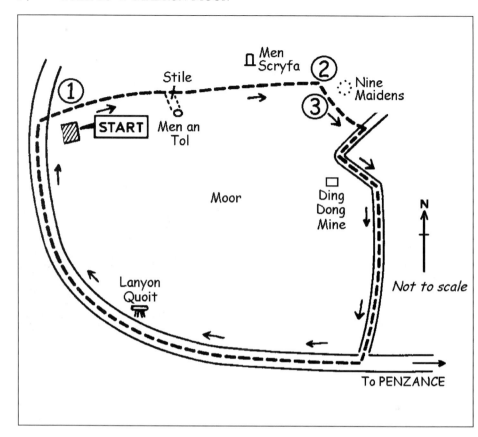

Megalithic Quoits, which are massive stones standing upright with a covering capstone although they were originally covered with soil.

An unusual monument, known as the Men an Tol (Cornish for 'Stone with a Hole') consists of two upright stones separated by one with a hole through the middle. Stone circles are classed as Megalithic monuments and, as the name suggests, are a circle of any number of rough-hewn upstanding stones. The purpose of these circles is obscure but the general belief that they were used for religious or ceremonial purposes is the most likely one. Standing stones, seen all over the county, are usually placed as waymarks and in some cases (as in the one on this moor) as memorial stones to a chieftain. Men Scryfa, Cornish for the 'Stone with Writing', can be seen during this walk as can Lanyon Quoit, just off the road on the return journey.

THE WALK
❶ Follow the clearly defined track to the Men an Tol which lies just to the right of it. Return to the track continuing to a meeting of paths. If you wish to pay a visit to Men Scryfa then turn left here. You will

Walkers on Madron Moor

soon see this impressive standing stone. Return to the track and continue to a junction of paths. Continue straight ahead for a short distance then turn right.

❷   Now follow a path across the moor. You are making for a derelict mine engine house on the brow of the hill. Leave the main path

---

FOOD and DRINK

In Madron village you will find the King William IV Inn, a good spot to stop for refreshments. Telephone: 01736 363022. During the summer months, a studio/tearoom is open opposite the layby at the start of the walk.

---

if you wish to see the stone circle known as the Nine Maidens. This is off to the left. You should be able to see it from the path. There always seems to be a feeling of mystery about this place!

❸   Return to the path and continue to the engine house. Join a track and turn to the right. This rather rough track soon meets a tarmac roadway with Bosiliak Farm on the right. From here continue until you meet the road from Madron. Turn right. In about half a mile look for Lanyon Quoit on the right with a layby and steps over a wall. Continue on this road back to your starting point, passing Lanyon Farm as you go.